LIST OF FREEMEN OF MASSACHUSETTS, 1630-1691

LUCIUS R. PAIGE

With an Index by
Elizabeth Petty Bentley

CLEARFIELD

Originally published in
The New England Historical and Genealogical Register
III, January, April, July, October 1849
as "List of Freemen"

Consolidated and reprinted
under a new title and with a new index
Genealogical Publishing Co., Inc.
Baltimore, 1978, 1980, 1988

Reprinted for
Clearfield Company, Inc. by
Genealogical Publishing Co., Inc.
Baltimore, Maryland
1998, 2002

Library of Congress Catalogue Card Number 78-50979
International Standard Book Number: 0-8063-0806-0

Made in the United States of America

NOTICES CONCERNING THE EARLY "FREEMEN" IN NEW ENGLAND.

Before a member of society could exercise the right of suffrage, or hold any public office, he must be made a *freeman* by the general or quarterly court. To become such he was required to produce evidence that he was a respectable member of some Congregational church. "This regulation was so far modified by Royal order in 1664, as to allow individuals to be made Freemen, who could obtain certificates of their being correct in doctrine and conduct, from clergymen acquainted with them."*

"In 1631, a test was invented which required all freemen to be church-members. This was upon the first appearance of a dissent in regard to religious opinions. But even this test, in the public opinion, required great caution, as in 1632 it was agreed that a civil magistrate should not be an elder in the church."†

The "FREEMAN'S OATH" was the first paper printed in New England. It was printed at Cambridge, by STEPHEN DAYE, in 1639,‡ upon a single sheet, in the manner of a handbill, and without date. It was in these words, as established in 1634 : —

I (*A. B.*) being by Gods providence, an Inhabitant, and Freeman, within the Jurisdiction of this Commonwealth; do freely acknowledge my self to be subject to the Government thereof: And therefore do here swear by the great and dreadful Name of the Ever-living God, that *I* will be true and faithfull to the same, and will accordingly yield assistance & support thereunto, with my person and estate, as in equity *I* am bound; a.id will also truly endeavor to maintain and preserve all the liberties and priviledges thereof, submitting my self to the wholesome Lawes & Orders made and established by the same. And further, that *I* will not plot or practice any evill against it, or consent to any that shall so do; but will timely discover and reveal the same to lawfull Authority now here established, for the speedy preventing thereof.

Moreover, *I* doe solemnly bind my self in the sight of God, that when I' shal be called to give my voyce touching any such matter of this State, in which Freemen are to deal, *I* will give my vote and suffrage as I shall judge in mine own conscience may best conduce and tend to the publike weal of the body, So help me God in the Lord Jesus Christ.§

The first General Court in Massachusetts was held on the 19th of October, 1630, not by representatives, but by every one that was free, of the corporation, in person. None had been admitted *freemen* since they left England. It was ordered, that for the future the *free-*

---

* Felt, *Hist. of Ipswich*, 18.
† Bentley, *Description of Salem*, 1 *Colls. Mass. Hist. Soc.*, vi. 236.
‡ Thomas, *Hist. Printing*, i. 231.
§ Copied from "New England's JONAS *cast up at* London," "by Major *John Childe*," 1647. [In the body of the tract the name of *Childe* is spelt without the *e*.] Mr. Felt has also printed the oath in his *Ipswich*, from the records, and it is likewise to be found in the " *Charters and Laws of Massachusetts Bay.*" We have copied from MAJOR CHILDE to preserve the old orthography.

3

men should choose the assistants, and the assistants from among themselves choose the governor and deputy governor. The court of assistants were to have the power of making laws and appointing officers. This was a departure from their charter. *One hundred and nine* freemen were admitted at this court. MAVERICK, BLACKSTONE, and many more who were not of any of the churches, were of this number. The next General Court was the court of election for 1631. The scale was now turned, and the *freemen* resolved to choose both governor, deputy, and assistants, notwithstanding the former vote, and made an order, that, for the time to come, none should be admitted to the freedom of the body politic but such as were church members.* "None have voice in elections of Governor, Deputy and Assistants, none are to be Magistrates, Officers or Jurymen, grand or petit, but *Freemen.* The Ministers give their votes in all elections of Magistrates. Now the most of the persons at *New England* are not admitted of their Church, and therefore are not *Freemen;* and when they come to be tried there, be it for life or limb, name or estate, or whatsoever, they must be tried and judged too by those of the Church who are, in a sort, their adversaries; How equal that hath been or may be, some by experience doe know, others may judge."†

"This," remarks Hutchinson, "was a most extraordinary order of law, and yet it continued in force until the dissolution of the government, it being repealed, in appearance only, after the restoration of King Charles the Second. Had they been deprived of their civil privileges in England by an act of parliament, unless they would join in communion with the churches there, it might very well have been the first in the roll of grievances. But such were the requisites to qualify for church membership here, that the grievance was abundantly greater."

It is supposed by Mr. Savage,‡ that "near three fourths of the present [1826] inhabitants of the six New England states," are descended from such as were made freemen before the death of Governor Winthrop. This conjecture would seem plausible enough were we to end our inquiries here; but if we extend them to the revolution of 1688, the time when the practice of making freemen ceased, by a similar course of reasoning we should not *now* find inhabitants enough in New England for our purpose. However, our opinion is, that from the "OLD FREEMEN" before the Revolution, *above seven eighths* of all the present inhabitants of New England, and no inconsiderable portion of those of New York, New Jersey, Pennsylvania, and Ohio are descended.

In 1663, "the practice of freemen's meeting in Boston to elect magistrates was repealed. This repeal, however, was so unpopular, that the same practice was renewed the next year; but it seems to have gone down soon after. At first, danger from Indians was pleaded, why

---

* Hutchinson's *Hist. Mass.,* i. 25, 26.
† Lechford, *Plain Dealing,* 23, 24.
‡ Winthrop, *Jour.,* ii. 74. In his edition of this invaluable work, Mr. S. has printed lists of the FREEMEN to the time of his author's death.

border and distant towns should, retain part of their freemen from General Election. At last, the greatness of the number, when assembled from the whole colony to choose the magistrates, and the concurrent inconveniencies of this custom, appear to have been the cause of producing an alteration, which substantially accords with present usage."*

At as early a day as practicable, it is intended that the most perfect list of FREEMEN possible to be obtained shall occupy a prominent space in our pages. At present we can give only a few items, enough, however, for our students to form some opinion of what the undertaking will be to do the OLD FREEMEN justice. It is proposed here to notice only such as offered themselves for freemen, or such of them as have come to our knowledge in a single year, viz :—

1677.

The : 22 : 3 : 77. These may Certifye the much honred Generall Court sitting at Boston the : 23. of the : 3. 77 : that the psons Whose names ar vnder wretten being in full communion with the Church of christ in Medffeild and otherwise quallified according to Law Desire that they may be admited to the ffredom of this Comon Welth.

> Obediah Morse   Edward Adams
> Jonathn Morse   Eliezur Adams
> Joseph Bullin
>
>   p George Barbur.

May 23 1677. This may signify to whom it may Concern y^t
> Mr. Richard Dumer &
> Mr. Henry Shorte

are members in full Comunion wth ye Church of Newbury as affirms
>   Jn° Richardson *Minister.*

---

1. 4: 77.   ffranses ffletcher
>   Timothy Wheeler
>   John Meriam
>   Samuel Jones

are in full communion with the Churche at Concord as attests
>   John fflint.

June 9th 1677.+† Mr. John Holyoke of Springfeild a member of ye church there in full comunion : a householder & above 24. yeare of age desires to be admitted to ye freedome of this Collony   attested
>   John Pynchon.

---

‡ These psons are in full Comunion with the Church of Christ in Wooburn desiring their freedome
> John Walker
> John Carter
> John Berbeane

[On the same paper.] James Blake in full Comunion with ye church in Dorchester & 24 years of age.   [No signature.

---

* Felt, *Ipswich*, 18, 19. See, also, *Annals of Salem*, 219, 220.
† This mark is on the original paper, but why is not fully apparent.
‡ The following entries are without date, but are believed to be all of 1677

Steuen Greenlef Junir
Jacob tapin
Retcherd bartlet Junir
these are Members of the Churtch of Nubery in full Comunion.
[No signature.]

John Eaton
Samuel Lamson
Henery Merow
Sebred Tailor
These are members in full Comunion in ye Church of Redding.
[No signature.]

The names of such as Are in full Communion with the Church of Christ in Charlstowne: for freedom

Mr. Samuell Nowell
Mr. John Phillips
Christofer Goodin
James Millar
Mr. John Blaney.   [No signature.]

Samuell Stodder
Andrew lane
John tucker
Are members of the Church of Hingham in full Comunion desire to be freemen.   [No signature.]

Joseph Parmeter
a householder & member of the Church of Brantry in full Comunion Desires to be a freeman of this Comonwealth.
[In another hand.]   Samuel Wintworth
a householder & in full comunion with ye Church of Douer desires the ffreedom of this comon wealth.   [No signature.]

John Wales Senior
A member of the Church of Christ in Dorchester desires his freedome.*
[In another hand.]   John White sen^r
of Muddy Riuer [now Brookline] being in full Comunion with the Church of Roxbury desiereth his Freedom.   [No signature.]

Salem   Mr. Jn° Hathorne
               Manasser Marsten
               Henry Skery Jun
all in full Comunion.   [No signature.]

* A cross stands in the margin against both these entries. They signified, probably, that the matter of each had been disposed of or acted upon.

The names of those men which desiar to tak ther freedum
Nathaniell Gay*   William Auery
Thomas Aldridge   Jonathan Auery
Nathaniell Kingsbery   John Weare
these ar all members in full Comunion in Dedham Church as attest
                                   Daniell ffisher

John Rogers
John Baylie
are householders & members of the Church of Waymouth in full Communion desire the freedome of this Comon wealth.
                    p'sented by the Deputy of y^t Towne

Members of the of ye first Church [Boston] To be made ffree
William Gibson
Nathaniell Barnes
Edward Ashley
   of ye North Church
Theophilus Thornton
John Jonse [Jones.]

In the above collection of applicants for *freedom* it is not certain that
we have all or any considerable part of those who did apply. Such are
given as happened to be within our reach. They may, however, be all
that applied in the year 1677 at the General Court. The number ap-
plying at the Quarterly County Courts may have been much greater.
From hence some notion may be gathered of what the number of freemen may have amounted to in the course of *fifty-seven years.* From
1630 to 1648, there are recorded† *one thousand eight hundred and*
nine. This number arose through a course of *eighteen years.*
   At some future time, as already hinted, we intend to give as full a
list of the early FREEMEN of New England as we can procure. Mean-
time our correspondents are requested to consider this a direct call
upon them to help us in this CORNER STONE of our New England history.

LIST OF FREEMEN.

[Communicated by Rev Lucius R. Paige of Cambridge, member of the N. E. Hist. Geneal. Society.]

Under the first charter of the Massachusetts colony, none were regarded as freemen, or members of the body politic, except such as were admitted by the General Court and took the oath of allegiance to the government here established. This custom continued in existence until, by the second charter, the colony was transformed into a province. Mr. Savage, in his edition of Winthrop's Journal, published a list of persons admitted freemen, up to May 10, 1648; and he justly remarked, that "these are probably ancestors of near three fourths of the present inhabitants of the six New England states, with almost half of New York and Ohio." Having occasion to use a more full list of freemen, I transcribed, nearly eight years ago, the names of all the persons admitted freemen, up to the time when the practice was discontinued, as recorded in the office of the Secretary of State. Agreeably to the request of the editor of the Register, this list is now furnished for publication. The names stand in the same order as in the original, and the orthography is carefully preserved. To guard more effectually against mistakes, I have recently, after so long an interval, compared my copy with the original, and I believe it to be correct, so far as the original remains legible. It is not surprising that many of the names are incorrectly spelled. They are not autographs; but they were written by the Secretary, according to the sound, as the names were pronounced to him. Moreover, it sometimes occurred, doubtless, that he did not catch the sound accurately, and therefore mistook the true name. I have endeavoured to exhibit an exact transcript; so that all readers may have the same opportunity to make proper corrections, which a perusal of the original would afford.

The oath administered to freemen is a document not without interest, and is here inserted, both in its original and its revised form, the orthography only being changed.

" The oath of a Freeman, or of a man to be made Free.

"I, A. B. &c. being by the Almighty's most wise disposition become a member of this body, consisting of the Governor, Deputy Governor, Assistants and Commonalty of the Massachusetts in New England, do freely and sincerely acknowledge that I am justly and lawfully subject to the Government of the same, and do accordingly submit my person and estate to be protected, ordered and governed by the laws and constitutions thereof, and do faithfully promise to be from time to time obedient and conformable thereunto, and to the authority of the said Governor and Assistants, and their successors, and to all such laws, orders, sentences and decrees as shall be lawfully made and published by them or their successors. And I will always endeavor (as in duty I am bound) to advance the peace and welfare of this body or commonwealth, to my utmost skill and ability. And I will, to my best power and means, seek to divert and prevent whatsoever may tend to the ruin or damage thereof, or of any the said Governor, Deputy Governor, or Assistants, or any of them, or their successors, and will give speedy notice to them, or some of them, of any sedition, violence, treachery, or other hurt or evil, which I shall know, hear, or vehemently suspect, to be plotted or intended against the said commonwealth, or the said Government established. And I will not, at any time, suffer or give consent to any counsel or attempt, that shall be offered, given, or attempted, for the impeachment of the said Government, or making any change or alteration of the same, contrary to the laws and ordinances thereof; but shall do my utmost endeavor to discover, oppose and hinder all and every such counsel and attempt. So help me God." — *Col. Rec. Vol. I. page* 1.

"At a General Court holden at Boston, May 14, 1634.

"It was agreed and ordered, that the former oath of freemen shall be revoked, so far as it is dissonant from the oath of freemen hereunder written; and that those that received the former oath shall stand bound no further thereby, to any intent or purpose, than this new oath ties those that now take the same." *

19 Oct. 1630.   The names of such as desire to be made ffreemen.

Mr. Sam¹¹ Mav'acke
Mr. Edw. Johnson
Mr. Edw. Gibbins
Mr. Will. Jeffries
Mr. John Burslin
Mr. Sam¹¹ Sharpe
Mr. Tho. Graves
Mr. Roger Conant
John Woodbury
Peter Palfry
Mr. Nath. Turner
Mr. Sam¹¹ ffreeman
Eprahim Childe
Mr. Willm Clerke
Mr. Abraham Palmer
John Page
Mr. Robte ffeake
Mr. Willm Pelham
Mr. Ben. Brand
Mr. Will: Blackstone
Mr. Edmond Lockwood
Mr. Rich. Browne
John Stickland
Ralfe Sprage
Mr. George Ludlowe
James Peñ   (62)
Henry Woolcott
Thomas Stoughton
Willm Phelpes
George Dyar
John Hoskins
Thomas fford
Nich. Upsall
Stephen Terree
Henry Smyth
Roger Willms
John Woolridge
Tho. Lumberd
Bigatt Egglestone
John Grinoway
Christopher Gibson
John Benham
Thomas Willms als. Harris
Rich., Garrett

John Howman
John Crabb
Capt. Walt' Norton
Mr. Alex. Wignall
Mr. Willm Jennison
Mr. Thomas Southcoate
Mr. Rich. Southcoate
James Pemb'ton
Mr. John Dillingham
John Johnson
George Alcocke
Mr. Robte Coles
John Burr
Thomas Rawlins
Rich. Bugby
Rich. Hutchins
Ralfe Mushell
Thomas Lambe
Will: Throdingham
Willm Chase
    ffoxewell
Mr. Charles Gott
Henry Harwood
Mr. George Phillips
Mr. John Wilson
Mr. John Mav'acke
Mr. John Warham
Mr. Sam¹¹ Skelton
Mr. Will. Colbron
Mr. Will. Aspinwall
Edw. Converse
Mr. Rich. Palgrave
John Taylour
Rich. Church
Rich. Silvester
Will. Balstone
Robte Abell
Mr. Giles Sexton
Robte Seely
John Mills
John Cranwell
Mr. Ralfe Glover
Willm Hulberd
Edmond James

John Pillips
Nath. Bowman
John Doggett
Laurence Leach
Daniel Abbott
Charles Chadwicke
Will. Drakenbury
John Drake
John Balshe
Mr. Sam¹¹ Coole
Mr. Will. Traske
Will. Gallard
Will. Rockewell
Henry Herricke
Sam¹¹ Hosier
Rich. Myllett
Mr. Abraham Pratt
Willm James
Willm Allen
Sam¹¹ Archer   (68)
Col. Rec., Vol. I. pp. 62, 63.

18 May 1631.

The names of such as took the oath of ffreemen.

Mr. John Mav'acke
Mr. Jo: Warham
Mr. Willm Blackestone
Mr. George Phillips
Mr. Rich. Browne
Capt. Dan¹¹ Pattricke
Capt. Jo: Und'hill
Capt.   Southcoate
Mr. Tho. Graves
Capt. Walt' Norton
Mr. George Throckm'ton
Mr. Wm. Colbran
S'ieant   Morris
S'ieant   Stickland
Mr. Roger Conant
Mr. Charles Gott
Ralfe Sprage
Laurence Leach
John Horne

* See page 3.

Mr. Sam^{ll} Coole
John Woodbury
Mr. John Oldeham
Edmond Lockewood
John Page
Mr. Rich. Palgrave
John Doggett
Rich. Sprage
ffraunes Johnson
Tho. Stoughton
Abraham Palmer
John Johnson
Robte Coles, — erased in
    the record.
Eprahim Childe
Bray Rossiter
Robte Seely
Biggott Egglestone
Mr. Will. Clearke
Willm Noddle
Mr. Robte ffeakes
Willm. Agar
Nich Stower
John Benham
Willm Balstone
Stephen Terre
Sam^{ll} Hosier
Robte Hardinge
Willm Woods
Mr. George Alcocke
Robte Moulton
Pet' Palfry
Mr. Edw. Belchar
John Edmonds
George Phillips
Roger Willms
John Balche
John Moore
Henry Herricke
John Hoskins
Math. Grant
John Burr
Simon Hoytt
Charles Chadwicke
Willm Parks
Ralfe Mushell
Willm Hudson
Walt' Palmer
Henry Smyth
Tho. fford
Jonas Weede
Mr. Edw. Tomlyns
Mr. Rich. Saltonstall
Edw. Gibbons
Mr. Alex. Wignall
Mr. Willm Gennison
Dan^{ll} Abbott
Tho. Rawlins
Rich. Bugby
John Warren

Mr. Willm Jeffry
Davy Johnson
Nich. Upsall
Willm Bateman
Dan^{ll} ffinch
Mr. Jo. Burslyn   (73)
Mr. John Maisters
John Peirce
Griffin Crofte
George Dyar
Willm Rockewell
Tho. Moore
John Taylour
Ezekiell Richardson
Edw. Converse
Robte Abell
Mr. John Dillingham
Isaacke Sterne
Roger Mawry
Tho. Dexter, — erased in
    the record.
Tho. Lambe
Tho. Willms
John fferman
John Gosse
John Grinnoway
Gyles Sexton
Tho. Lumberd
Mr. Edw. Jones
Willm Gallerd
Willm Allen
Rich. Bulgar
Rich. ffoxewell
Willm. ffelpes
John Perkins
Mr. Sam^{ll} Skelton
Mr. Edw. Johnson
Wm. Cheesebrough
Anthony Dixe
ffraunes Smyth
ffrauncis Aleworth   (74)
    C. R., Vol. I. pp. 73, 74.

    March 6, 1631-2.

Mr. John Ellyott
Jacob Ellyott
Abraham Browne
James Pennyman
Isaack Perry
Gregory Baxter
Willm ffrothingham
Sam^{ll} Moore
John Blacke
John Mylls
    C. R., Vol. I. p. 74.

    April 3, 1632.

Mr. John Winthrop jun'
Mr. Willm Aspinwall
John Sampeford

Willm Hulbert
    C. R., Vol. I. p. 74.

    July 3, 1632.

Mr. Nath. Turner
John Ruggles
Elias Stileman
Mr. Willm Dennison
Mr. Sam^{ll} Sharpe
Mr. John Wilson
John Moore
    C. R., Vol. I. p. 74.

    August 7, 1632.

John Phillips
Valentine Prentice
John Hull
Sam^{ll} Wakeman
    C. R , Vol. I. p. 74

    Oct. 2, 1632.

Mr. Sam^{ll} Mav'icke
    C. R., Vol. I. p. 74.

    Nov. 6, 1632.

Mr. Tho. Weld
Mr. Tho. James
Mr. Jo. Willust
Mr. Jo. Coggeshall
Mr. Rich. Dumer
Mr. Tho. Ollyver
Mr. John Branker
Mr. Tho. Beecher
Tho. ffrench
Willm Goodwin
John Beniamin
John Talcott
James Olmstead
John Clerke
Willm Leawis
Nath. Richards
Willm Wadsworth
Rich. Webb
    C. R., Vol. I. p. 74.

    March 4, 1632-3.

Willm Curtis
Thomas Uffott
John Perry
Isaack Morrall
Willm Heath
George Hull
Eltweed Pummery
Nich. Denselow
Gyles Gibbs
John Neweton
John White
Willm Spencer
John Kirman
Tymothy Tomlyns   (74)

Henry Harwood
Richard Collocott
Willm Brakenbury
John Smyth   (79)
  C. R., Vol. I. pp. 74, 79.

April 1, 1633.
S'ieant Greene
Rise Coles
Willm Dady
  C. R., Vol. I. p. 79.

June 11, 1633.
Willm Stilson
Rich. Millett
Rich. Lyman
Jes'' Rawling
Tho. Smyth
David Wilton
John Witchfield
Elias Mav'acke
  C. R., Vol. I. p. 79.

Nov. 5, 1633.
Mr. Israell Stoughton
Mr. John Coggin
Mr. Willm Hill
Mr. John Moody
John Porter
ffrauncis Weston
John Watson
John Holgrave
  C. R., Vol. I. p. 79.

March 4, 1633-4.
Thomas Grubb
Edmond Hubbert
Edw. Hutchingson
Mr. Tho. Leveritt
Mr. Gyles fferman
Edmond Quinsey
Willm Collishawe
Thomas Minor
Tho. Howlett
John Gage
Sam'' Wilboare
John Levens
John Cranwell
Edw. Mellowes
James Browne
Mr. John Woolridge
Josuah Hewes
Robte Turner
John Biggs
Tho. Matson
Walter Merry
Rich. Tappin
Mr. Atterton Hough
Willm Andrewes
Rich. Walker
George Ruggles

Mr. Nich. Parker.
  C. R., Vol. I. p. 79.

April 1, 1634.
Mr. Dan'' Dennison
George Minott
Rich. Gridley
Thomas Reade
George Hutchingson
Robte Roise
John Pemerton
Bernard Lumbert
Henry Wulcott
Rich. Hull
John Gallop
Richard Silvester
Willm Horseford
  C. R., Vol. I. p. 79.

May 14, 1634.
John Haynes Esq.
Phillip Sherman
Daniell Brewer
Tho. Gaildthait
Robte Gamlyn Sen'
Thomas Hale
Edward Riggs
John Walker
Thomas Wilson
Sam'' Basse
Tho. Pigg
Willm Hill
Sam'' ffinch
George Williams
Edw. Gyles
Willm Dixy
George Norton
Thomas Eborne
Dan'' Wray
Abraham Mellowes
John Ollyver
Robte Hale
Tho. Cakebread   (79)
Tho. Squire
Robte Houlton
John Odlyn
Roger Clapp
Josuah Carter
Thomas Talmage
Richard ffairebancks
Phillip Tabor
Gregory Taylour
John Chapman
Willm Learned
Mr. Tho. Hooker
Mr. Sam'' Stone
Edw. Howe
Bartholmewe Greene
Rich. Wright
John Steele
Edm. Stebbins

Andrewe Warner
George Steele
Rich. Butlar
Thomas Spencer
Edw. Muste
Rich. Goodman
John Pratt
John Haward
Andrewe Ward
Joseph Twitchwell
Tho. Hatch
George Whitehand
Jerad Hadden
Joseph Reddings
Anthony Colby
John Bosworth
ffrauncis Plumer
Humfry Pynny
Bray Wilkins
James Rawlyns
Jacob Barny
Tho. Lowthrop
Steven Hart
Jeffery Massy
Rich. Brakenbury
Tho. ffaireweath'
Willm Hedges
John Hoskins
Peter Woolfe
Willm Chase
Willm Talmidge
Mr. John Cotton
Nath. Gillett
Dan'' Howe
Myles Reddin
John Eales
Mr. Willm Peirce
Mr. Tho. Mahewe
Robte Walker
Phillipp Randill
Tho. Holcombe
Tho. Dewey
Tho. Jeffry
James Parker
Walter ffiler
John Haydon
Edmond Harte
Willm Hathorne
Steven ffrench
Christopher Hussey
Edw. Bendall
John Button
Rich. Raymond
Jonathan Wade
Tho. Coldham
James Tompson
Tho. Hubbard
John Hall
John Baker
Mr. Willm Brenton
John Capen

ffrauncis Dent
Henry ffeakes (112)
C. R., Vol. I. pp. 79, 112.

Sep. 3, 1634.
Beniamin Hubbard
Edmond Hubbard
John Mousell
Willm Baker
Willm Nashe
Thomas Goble
Ollyver Mellowes
Robte Gamlyne
Ralfe Hiningway
Jesᵖʳ Rawlyns
John Stowe
John Cumpton
Willm ffreeborne
Willm Perkins
James Everill
Jonathan Negos
Nicholas Willust
Alex. Becke
Henry Pease
Samˡˡ Crumwell
Joseph Rednape
Edw. Hutchingson
John Sibley
Hugh Hillyard
Moses Mavʳacke
Mr. John Spencer
Robte Mussey
Henry Shorte
Phillip ffowler
Bryan Pendleton
Abraham ffinch
Anthony Peirce
John Bernard
Martyn Undʳwood
Samˡˡ Smyth
John Browne
John Edy
Robte Abbitt
Robte Coe
Nathanell ffoote
Rich. Davenport
Mr. Tho. Newbery
John Pope
John Hawkes
Ralfe ffogg
Robert Reynolls
Robte Potter
John Hardy
Thomas Thorneton
Matthias Sension
Mr. Tho. Parker
Mr. Nicholas Easton
Mr. James Noise
Josuah Hubbard
C. R., Vol. I. p. 113.

March 4, 1634–5.
Capt. John Mason
Hugh Mason
George Munings
John Brandishe
Samˡˡ Hubbert
Edward Dixe
Thomas Bartlett
George Buncar
Robte Blott
Rich. Kettle
Willm Johnson
Thomas Lynd
Mr. Willm Andrewes
Willm Westwood
Mathewe Allen
Guy Bambridge
Willm Pantry
Tho. ffisher
John Hopkins
John Bridge
Willm Kelsey
John Bernard
James Ensigne
Samˡˡ Greenehill
Tymothy Stanley
Rich. Lord
John Prince
Edw. Winshipp
Samˡˡ Greene
Joseph Clerke
John Wulcott
Abraham Newell
Rich. Pepper
Isaac Johnson
Christopher Peake
Thomas Woodford
Thomas Scott
Tho. Boreman
Roger Lanckton
John Webster
Hugh Sheratt
Joseph Metcalfe
Will. Bartholmewe
Tho. Dorman
Rich. Kent
James Davis
John Newegate
Mr. Will. Hutchingson
Tho. Marshall
Rich. Cooke
Willm Nethʳland
Tho. Wardall
Rich. Hutchingson
ffr. Hutchingson
Gamaliell Wate
Rich. Trusedale
Edw. Hitchin
Robte Parker
Joseph Easton

John Tylley
Tho. Stanley
C. R., Vol. I p. 113.

May 6, 1635.
Philemon Portmorte
Henry Elkines
Christ. Martial
Edmond Bulckley
Eward Browne
Jarrett Bourne
Willm Pell
Beniamyn Gillom
Tho. Alcocke
Edmonde Jacklinge
John Sebley
Tho. Peirce
Mr. Sachariah Syms
Barnaby Wynes
Jeffery fferris
John Reynolls
Henry Bright
Tho. Hastings
John Lethermore
John Batchelʳ
John Tompson
John Clerke
Tho. Swifte
Robte Wincall
Tho. Hosmer
Willm Butlar
John Arnoll
George Stockin
Nathanaell Ely
Robte Day
Jerymy Adams
Joseph Maggott
John Hall
Samˡˡ Allen
Humfry Bradstreete
Thomas Pyne
John Gay
George Strange
Nathanaell Duncan
Thomas Marshall
Thomas Hoskins
Richard Kemball
Robte Andrewes
Henry Wright
Jonathan Jellett
Tho. Gun
Robte Dibell
Henry ffowkes
Elias Parkeman
John Blackeleach
Danˡˡ Morse
Joseph Morse
Edward Garfield
Rich. Browne
Willm Moody

14   *List of Freemen.*

Christ. Osgood
Tho. Buckland
Richard Jacob
Aron Cooke
George Phelpes
Boniface Burton
Robte Bootefishe
Robte Dryver
Willm Edmonds
John Ravensdale
John Legg
George ffarr
Robte Cotty
Mr. Steven Batchel^r
C. R., Vol. I. p. 153.

Sep. 2, 1635.

Willm Blumfeild
Joseph Hull
Willm Reade
Richard Adams
John Upham
Robte Lovell
Willm Smyth
Richard Woodward
Peter Hubbert
Mr. George Byrditt
Mr. Townsend Bishopp
Phillip Vereing
Mr. John ffawne
Thomas Scraggs
C. R., Vol. I. p. 153.

March 3, 1635–6.

Mr. Clem^t. Chaplaine
Willm Mosse
Willm Dyar
Joseph Wells
John Cogeswell
Richard Tuttle
Robte Lord
Willm Walton
Tho. Loreing
Clem^t Bates
John Astwood
Tho. Wakely
Willm Norton
George Ludkin
George Marshe
John Ottis
Nicholas Baker
Nicholas Jacob
David Phippin
Edmond Batter
Philemon Dolton
John Whitney
Willm Swayne
Henry Kingman
Thomas White
Angell Hollard
John Kingsbury

John Levett
Tho. Rawlyns
Roger Harlakendine Esq.
Mr. Joseph Cooke
Mr. George Cooke
Mr. Nich. Danforth
Tho. Marryott
Mr. Sam^{ll} Shepheard
Willm ffrench
Simon Crosby
Tho. Cheeseholme
John Russell
Passevell Greene
Mr. Hugh Peters
Thomas Bloyett
Edmond ffrost
Mr. Tho. Shepheard
Henry Vane Esq.
Tho. Ewer
Tho. Brigden
Michaell Bastowe
Joseph Andrewes
C. R., Vol. I. p. 153.

May 25, 1636.

Jasper Gun
Thom: Bell
Mr. Samuell Apleton
Isaack Heathe
Philip Elliot
Adam Mott
William Webbe
Edward Woodman
Thomas Judd
John Knight
Rich'd Knight
Anthony Mosse
Rob't Longe
Rob't Hawkins
Edward Carington
Bernard Capen
Will. Hamond
John Saunders
Robert Kaine
Daniel Maude
Ralph Hudson
Thomas Hassord
James Johnson
John Davy
George Bate
Nathaniell Heaton
Will. Benseley
Will. Townsend
Rich'd Bracket
Thom. Savage
Mr. Henry fflinte
Will. Courser
James Browne
Zacheus Bosworth
Mathias Ives
Will. Wilson

Will. Salter
Anthony Harker
Edward Goffe
Rich'd Champnyes
Edmond Lewis
John Stowers
John Smythe
John Eaton
Edmond Sherman
John Coolidge
Gregory Stone
Symon Stone
George Hepburne
Will. Kinge
Augustine Clement
Rich'd Karder
John Higgenson
John Mylam
Thom. Dimocke
John Loverin
Willi. Wilcocks
Edward Bennet
Thom. Mekyn junior
Hugh Gunnison
Edmond Jackson
Bernaby Doryfall
Mr. Rich'd Bellingham
Mr. John Winthrope sen.
Mr. John Humfrey
Mr. Thom. Dudley
Mr. Will. Coddington
Increase Nowell
Symon Bradstreete
C. R., Vol. I. p. 194.

Dec. 7, 1636.

James Bate
Edward Clapp
John Smythe
Edward White
David Price
George Aldridge
Oliver Purchase
John Webbe
Alexand^r Winchester
Robert Scotte
Steven Winthrope
Will. Goodhewe
Gilbert Crackborne
Samuell Whiteing
Thomas Brooke
Willi. Wilcockson
Will. Beadseley
Alexand^r Knolls
Thom. Atkinson
John Holland
Walter Nicoles
C. R., Vol. I. p. 194.

Dec. 8, 1636.

Mr. Thom. Jenner

ffrancis Lightfoote
Edward Howe
John Cooper
John More
Thom. Beale
   C. R., Vol. I. p. 154.

March 9, 1636-7.

Edward Ketcham
Rich'd Roots
Joseph Isaack
John Hassell
Rich'd Betsham
Anthony Eames
Samuell Warde
Thomas Hamond
Thomas Underwood
Nicolas Hudson
John Winchester
Abraham Shawe
Rob't Lockwood
Will. Barsham
Rich'd Beares
Edward Bates
Jenkin Davies
Mathewe West
Gerret Spencer
Thomas Tylestone
Henry Collins
Robert Sedgwick
James Heyden
Thomas Samfoard
John Stronge
Thomas Carter
Joseph Armitage
Rich'd Wayte
Robert Hull
Rich. Wayde
Will. Dinny
Thomas Meakins
   C. R., Vol. I. p. 194.

April 18, 1637.

Thomas Parish
Thomas Briggam
William Cutter
Willi. Towne
John Gore
Robert Sever
John Ruggles
Laurence Whitamore
John Graves
Gyles Pason
George Kinge
   C. R., Vol. I. p. 195.

April 17, 1637.

Christopher ffoster
Thom. Browninge
Symon Eyre
William Dodge

ffrancis Smythe
Nathani. Porter
Edward Dinny
Willi. Dineley
ffranc' East
Nathani. Woodward
John Smythe
Edward Rainsfoard
Thomas Wheeler
John Laurence
   C. R., Vol. I. p. 195.

May 17, 1637.

Thom. Olney
Thom. Gardner
Joseph Pope
Willi. Bounde
Henry Bartholomewe
Joseph Grafton
ffrancis Skerry
Edmond Marshall
Henry Seawall junior
Henry Bull
Thomas Smythe
Nicolas Holt
Nicolas Noise
Archelaus Woodman
James Browne
John Bartlet
Robert Pike
Thomas Coleman
Mathewe Chafe
George Burden
George Hunn
Willi. Sumner
George Proctor
Thomas Millet
Thomas Dible
Philip Drinker
John Cheney
John Norton
John Syverens
Thom. Wells
John Perkins
Willi. Lampson
Thom. Bircher
Edward Porter
James Howe
Thom. Rogers
John Sharman
John Rogers
Myles Nutte
James Osmer
Rich'd Johnson
Thomas Parker
John Hanchet
John Gibson
   C. R., Vol. I. p. 195.

Sep. 7, 1637.

Mr. George Moxam

Mr. Tymo. Dalton
   C. R., Vol. I. p. 195.

Nov. 2, 1637.

Nathaniell Wales
Edw* Sale
Will. Casely
Mr. John ffiske
Mr. John Harvard
   C. R., Vol. I. p. 195.

March — 1637-8.

Thom. Spooner
Thomas Venner
James Moulton
James Haynes
Henry Skerry
Joseph Bachiler
John Symonds
John Gedney
Micha: Spencer
John Pearce
Nico. Busbey
Ralph Woodward
Samu. Symonds
Mr. Thom. fflint
Rich'd Griffinn
John Evert
George Haywood
Thom. ffoxe
George Hochens
Edward Rawson
Henry Rust
David ffiske
Willi. Harsye
Willi. Ludkin
Thom. Linkorne
Henry Tuttle
   C. R., Vol. I. p. 195.

May 2, 1638.

Samuell Rich'dson
Rob't Cutler
Thomas Rich'dson
Edward Johnson
John Brinsmeade
Isaack Mixer
Henry Kemball
Willi. Nickerson
Henry Dow
Nicho. Byram
Samu. Hackburne
Abraham Howe
John Tatman
Rob't Williams
Humfrey Atherton
Gabriell Meade
Ralph Tomkins
Rich'd Hawes
Alexander Miller
Joseph Wilson

Michaell Willes
John Sill
George Willis
Thomas Swetman
Edward Hall
Mr. William Hubberd
Rich'd Lumkin
Willi. Warrener
Marke Symonds
Thomas Rawlinson
Thomas Carter
Willi. Knight
George Taylor
John Gould
Thomas Cobbet
Daniell Peirce
Wi liam Ballard
Willi. Thorne
Abraham Tappin
Henry Lunt
John Browne
Henry Burdsall
    C. R., Vol. I. p. 196.
    June 9, 1638.
Mr. Natha. Eaton
    C. R., Vol. I. p. 196.
    Sep. 6, 1638.
The magistrates of Ipswich
  had order to give
Mr. Natha. Rogers the oath
  of Freedom.
    C. R., Vol. I. p. 196.
    Sep. 7, 1638.
Thomas Hale
Rich'd Singletery
Steven ffosditch
Nicholas Browne
Zachary ffitche
Thomas Tredwell
Geo. Giddings
    C. R., Vol. I. p. 196.
    March 13, 1638-9.
Mr. John Allen
Mr. Edward Alleyne
Mr. Ralph Wheelocke
Mr. Willm Tynge
John Leuson
John Frayrye
Eleazer Lussher
John Hunting
Rob't Hinsdall
Edward Kempe
John Dwite
Henry Phillips
Mr. Joseph Peck

Henry Smythe
Edward Gilman
Thomas Cooper
John Beale
Henry Chamberlin
Thomas Clapp
John Palmer
John Tower
Henry Webbe
James Mattucke
John Tuttle
Theophi. Wilson
Jeremy Belcher
Willi. Cockeram
Edward Bates
John Rogers
Christopher Batte
Samuel Neweman
Mr. Robert Peck
Edmond Greenliffe
Thomas Bulkeley
Luke Potter
Ephraim Wheeler
Robert Merriam
James Bennet
John Whiteman
William Palmer
William Eastowe
Thom. Moulton
Rich'd Swayne
Willi. Wakefeild
Thom. Joanes
    C. R., Vol. I. p. 196.
    March 14, 1638-9.
Nicho. Butler
Mr. Thom. Wills
Mr. Edward Holliock
Mr. Rich'd Sadler
Mr. Edward Howell
Thomas Townesend
Edward Baker
Henry Gaynes
Nicholas Batter
James Boutwell
Rich'd Wells
Willi. Langley
Robert Parsons
Godfrey Armitage
Arthur Geeree
Joseph Pell
Thomas Layton
Willi. Partridge
Roger Shawe
Robert Dannell
Hezechi. Upher
Christopher Cayne
Rob't Steedman
George Keezar

Edward Burcham
Joseph Merriam
Thomas Browne
George ffoule
Willi. Busse
Henry Brooke
Henry ffarewell
Roger Draper
John Miles
Sethe Switzer
Isaack Cole
John Wisewall
John Maudsley
Joseph ffarnworth
William Reed
William Blake
Thomas Dickerman
Thomas Clarke
"Mr. Endicot and Mr.
  John Winthrope jun. had
  order to give
Mr. Emanuel Downeing
  the oath of ffreedome."
    C. R., Vol. I. p. 196.
    22 May, 1639.
Mr. Willi. Sergent
Mr. Thom. Hawkins
Mr. Sam. ffreeman
Thomas Marten
Nichol. Guye
Mr. Samu. Winsley
Steven Dumer
John Osgood
John Gooffe
John Mussellwhit
Steven Kent
John Rimington
Thomas Browne
John Moulton
    Hulling
Rich' Waters
Thomas Ruggles
Joseph Shawe
ffrancis More
Walter Edmonds
Willi. Bowstreete
Hopestill ffostere
Thomas Scotto
Willi. Adams
Thomas Says
John Alderman
Griffin Bowen
John Spooer
Rich'd Hollidge
John Clarke
Giles ffirman
Josua Tedd
Beniamin ffelton

LIST OF FREEMEN.

22 May, 1639.
Jarvas Garfoard
Edward Breck
William Clarke
Edmond Bloise
Willi. Osborne
John Miller
George Holmes
Mathewe Boyse
James Astwood
John Rob't
Rich'd Pecocke
Edward Bridge
Walter Blackborne
Joseph Jewet
Roger Porter
Thomas ffirman
Natha. Chappell
John Skot
James Buck
Hugh Laskin
John Smythe
Henry Swan
    C. R., Vol. I. p. 254.

23 May, 1639.
Mr. Ezechi. Rogers
Mr. Natha. Rogers
Robert Saunders
Mr. Nathani. Sparhauke
Mr. Thom. Nelson
    C. R., Vol. I. p. 254.

6 June, 1639.
Steven Paine
James Garret
    C. R., Vol. I. p. 254.

6 Sep. 1639.
Mr. Thomas Ginner
Mr. Benia. Keayne
Job Swinnerton
William Lord
Laurence Southick
John Crosse
John Roffe
John Ellsley
Luke Hearde
Anthony Sadler
Thomas Masie
    C. R., Vol. I. p. 254.

7 Sep. 1639.
Edmond Bridge

Rich'd Mellen
Robert Tucke
Robert Saunderson
    C. R., Vol. I. p. 254.

13 May, 1640.
Mr. Willi. Worcester
Henry Munday
John Saunders
Thom. Bradberry
Thom. Dumer
Thoma. Barker
Thoma. Mighill
Maxami. Jewet
ffranc. Parrat
Rich'd Swan
Rob't Haseldine
John Haseldene
ffranc. Lambert
Willi. Scales
John Burbanke
Willi. Bointon
John Jarrat
Micha. Hopkinson
Geo. Kilborne
Mr. Thoma. Coytemore
Mr. Thoma. Graves
Mr. ffranc. Willoughby
Edward Larkin
Thom. Caule
John Penticus
John Martin
Willi. ffilllips
Abrah. Hill
Edward Woode
Willi. Paine
John Oliver (Newb')
James Standige
John Whipple
Mr. Edwa' Norrice
Mr. Thom. Ruck
Mr. Willi. Stevens
John ffairefeild
John Bachilor
Robert Elwell
Thom. Watson
Mark fformais
Thom. Waterhouse
Jeremy Howchenes
Jonas Humphryes
Thom. Toleman
George Weekes
John ffarnum
Rich'd Lipincote

Rich'd Withington
Rich'd Syckes
Clement Tapley
Gouin Anderson
John Bowelis
Edw'd Passon
Willi. Chanler
John Hall
John Trumbell
Edw⁴ Bumsted
Joseph Wheeler
Tymo. Wheeler
John Chaundler
Symon Rogers
Michaell Wood
John Merrill
George Browne
John Norwick
Edmo. Pitts
ffranc. Smyth
John Harding
Willi. Carpenter
John Holbroke
Nicho. ffilllipes
Thom. Bayly
Samu. Butterworth
Rob't Marten
Mathewe Prat
Rob't Tytus
Thom. Rich'ds
Henry Greene
Willi. Godfree
Thom. Arnall
Willi. Haward
Abra. Perkins
Jeffry Mingy
Arthur Clarke
James Davis
Mr. Edmond Browne
Peter Noyse
Walter Hayne
Edmond Rice
Thom. White
John Parmenter
John Bent
Edmond Goodnor
Thom. Islin
John Wood
John Ruddyk
John Howe
Mr. Willi. Hibbens
Arthur Perry
Valentine Hill
ffranc. Seyle

17

John Hurd
Natha. Williams
John Leveritt
Peter Oliver
John Kenerick
Antho. Stodard
Samu. Sherman
George Curtis
Cotten fflack
Mr. Willi. Tompson
George Rowes
Steven Kinseleye
John Dassette
Willi. Potter
Gregory Belchar
Thom. Place
James Copie
Thomas fflackman
Edward Spolden
Willi. Allise
Martin Saund's
John Read
Willi. Androws
John Stidman
Edmond Anger
Rich'd ffrances
John Thrumball
Willi. Manning
Edward Collins
Rich'd Hogg
Nathan Aldishe
Mychall Medcalfe
ffardinando Adams
ffranc. Chickering
Willi. Bullard
John Bullard
Henry Smythe
John Mose
Daniell ffisher
Josua ffisher
Rich'd Barbore
Jn°. Scarbrow
C. R., *Vol. I. p.* 281.

7 Oct. 1650.

Mr. Samu. Dudley
Josias Cobbitt
Edmond Gardner
James Barcker
Henry Sands
Rob't Hunter
Willi. Stickney
C. R., *Vol. I. p.* 281.

8 Oct. 1640.

John Page
Samu. Morse
Thomas Weight
C. R., *Vol. I. p.* 281.

9 Oct. 1640.

Rob't Ringe

Isaack Buswell
C. R., *Vol. I. p.* 281.
12 Oct. 1640.

Willi. Hudson
James Oliver
Thomas Painter
Edward ffletcher
Mr. Willi. Bellingham
Mr. Willi. Hooke
C. R., *Vol. I. p.* 281.

2 June 1641.

Mr. Henry Dunster
Mr. Rich'd Russell
Mr. John Allen
John Maies
Rich'd North
John Seir
John Stevens
Mr. Adam Winthrope
William Barnes
John Harrison
John Lowell
Thom. Davies
John Emery
Samu. Plumer
Moses Payne
Daniell Weld
Samu. Bidfeild
ffrancis Eliot
Abell Kelly
Jacob Wilson
Nicho. Woode
John Harbert
Thomas Lake
Andrew Pitcher
Rob't Holmes
Goulden More
Rich'd Cutter
John ffossenden
Willi. Woodberry
Willi. Geares
Philemon Dickenson
Esdras Reade
John Robinson
Thom. Gardner
Thom. Marston
Rich'd Bartelmew
Thom. Gould
Thom. Wildar
Rich'd Robinson
John Marston
Rob't ffuller
Willi. Blanchard
Bozoun Allen
Miles Ward
Samu. Corning
Jonathan Porter
Rich'd Pattinggell
John Goodnow
Willi. Browne

Samu. Chapun
Christo. Stanley
John Harrison
Thom. Davenish
Walter Harris
Ellis Barrone
Willi. Parker
Philip Veren
John Palmer
Rich'd Parker
Edw'd Tinge
Nehemi. Bourne
ffranc. Lawes
Rob't Bridges
John Baker
Rob't Cooke
Henry Dauson
Willi. Tiff
Willi. Brisco
Rich'd Sanford
Augustine Walker
Henry Archer
Charles Glover
Rob't Paine
John Baker
Micha. Katherick
John Jackson
John Deane
Edward Browne
Dani. Warner
John Knoulton
Symon Tompson
Rob't Daye
Andrewe Hodges
Jacob Leager
George Bullard
Henry Chick'y
Michaell Powell
Joseph Kingsberty
John Roaper
Nathani. Coalborne
John Elis
Edward Rich'ds
Beniamin Smyth
Austen Kilham
Thom. Payne
Tymo. Dwight
Henry Wilson
Samu. Bullen
Willi. ffuller
Willi. ff——
Evan Thomas
Abell Parr
Benia. Ward
Willi. Hunt
Willi. Bateman
Josias ffirman
Willi. Cop
Natha. Halsteed
Natha. Billing
Benia. Turney

Rich'd Rice
James Blood
Thom. Clarke
John Viall
Thom. Buttolph
ffranc. Douse
John Sweete
Arthur Gill
Thom. Clipton
George Merriam
John Heald
George Wheeler
Obedi. Wheeler
ffranc. Bloyce
　　C. R., Vol. I. p. 312.

4 June 1641.

Thom. Marshall
　　C. R., Vol. I. p. 312.

7 Oct. 1641.

Mr. Richard Blindman
Thomas Wheeler
　　C. R., Vol. I. p. 315.

18 May 1642.

Mr. ffrancis Norton
John Withman
Gawdy James
John March
Rob't Button
Benia. Vermaes
Thom. Antrum
Michaell Shaflin
Thom. Putman
John Cooke
Phineas ffiske
Willia. ffiske
James ffiske
George Byam
Rich'd Bishope
Allen Kenniston
Elias Stileman
John Tomkins sen'
Ananias Conkling
John Neale
John Bulfinch
Joseph Boyse
Samu. Grimes
Theodo. Atkinson
Rob't Bradford
Hugh Williams
Rich'd Crithley
John Guttering
John Ingoldsbey
Robert Howen
Thoma. Snowe
Thoma. ffoster
Dani. Briskow
John Search
John Baker
Rich'd Knight

Rich'd Tayler
Philip Tayler
John Bulkeloy
Edward Okes
Thom. Okes
Edward Gooding
Sampson Shore
Willi. Torry
John Coggan jnni.
John Clough
John Witherell
Samu. Thatcher
John Hill
Rich'd Wody
John Mathis
Willi. Lewes
Rich'd Taylor
Edward Carleton
Humphrey Reyn'
Hugh Smith
Hugh Chapline
Rich'd Lowden
John Burrage
Solomon Phips
John Greene
Isaack Comins
Allen Pearley
Thom. Thackster
Willi. Ripley
Mathewe Hawkes
Hugh Prichard
Thom. Lincolne
John Stoder
Willi. Robinson
Robert Peirce
Thom. Davenport
Rich'd Baker
Robert Pond
John Rigbey
George Right
Thom. Blisse
Benia. Albey
Roger Bancroft
Rich'd Eckels
John Cooper
John Tomkins jun'
Willi. Dickson
Moses Wheat
Rob't Edwards
Thomas Bateman
Willi. Aline
Thom Wheller
Willi. Hartwell
John Stevens
Willi. Stevens
Antho. Somersbey
Henry Somersbey
Willi. Berry
Samu. Guil
Abell Hews
John Swett

Peter Woodward
John Brock
Natha. Whiteing
Micha. Metcalfe
Rob't Page
ffranc. Pebody
Isaack Perkins
Thom. Worde
Henry Ambros
Walter Ropper
Henry Kibbey
David Zullesh
　　C. R., Vol. II. p. 18.

19 May 1642.

John Sadler
Walter Tybbot
Obedi. Brewer
Willi. Hilton
Willi. Walderne
　　C. R., Vol. II. p. 18.

22 June 1642.

Henry Palmer
Joseph Peaseley
Rich'd Pid
Willi. Titcombe
Willi. White
Thomas Dowe
　　C. R., Vol. II. p. 18.

2 August 1642.

Mr. Willi. Pinchen
　　C. R., Vol. II. p. 18.

14 Sept. 1642.

Thom. Het
　　C. R., Vol. II. p. 18.

21 Sept. 1642.

Will. English
　　C. R., Vol. II. p. 18.

27 Dec. 1642, At Salem,

Walter Price
Rob't Gutch
George Gardner
Rich'd Prence
Rob't Leoman
Thom. More
Thom. Tresler
Willi. Robinson
Hugh Cawkin
　　C. R., Vol. II. p. 18.

28 Feb. 1642–3.

Thom. Edwards
John Kitchin
Henry Harwood
　　C. R., Vol. II. p. 18.

28 Feb. 1642–3. At Salem·

Rich. More
Hugh Stacye

Thom. Avery
Edwᵃ. Beachamp
     C. R., Vol. II. p. 27.

10 May, 1643.

Mr. Thom. Wallis
John Scot
Isaack Wheeler
John Ward
Andrew Lister   (27)
Thom. Goodnow
Rob't Dants
Henry Looker
John Parmenter
Willi. Ward
John Newton
John Thurston
Christo. Smyth
John Guile
John Plunton
John Knights
John Jackson
Nathan ffiske
Geo. Parkhurst
John Pratt
Thom. Beard
John Arnol
John Hollister
James Prest
Nicho. White
Jeffry Turner
Willi. Turner
Roger Billindg
Laurence Smyth
Willi. Ware
Rich. Evans
Willi. Trescot
John Gurnell
Henry Woodworth
Nathani. How'd
Rich. Way
Rob. Williams
John Mansfeild
ffranc. James
Rob't Proctor
Willi. ffletchʳ
Willi. Vincen
John Woode
Hen. Bridgham
Rob't Mader
Geo. Barrell
Rich. Rawlen
Strong ffurnell
John Sand'bant
Isa. Colimer
Willi. Blanton
Miles Tarne
Natha. Norcros
James Morgan
Rob't Pepper
Rich. Hildrick

Edwᵃ Sheopard
Dan. Stone
Tho. Danforth
Andr. Stephenson
Willi. Manning
Henry Symons
John Tydd
John Wright
Benia. Butterfeild
Edwᵃ. Winn
Nicho. White
John Hollister
James Prest
John Albye
Peter Bracket
Natha. Herman
Sam. Adams
John Hastings
John Whetley
Willi. Phese
John Shephard
Tho. Adams   (28)
     C. R., Vol. II. pp. 27, 28.

29 May, 1644.

Cap. Dan. Gookens
ffaithfull Rouse
Rob't Leach
ffaintnot Wines
Willi. Bachiler
Willi. Smith
Willi. Green
Rob't ffeild
Thom. Marshall
Roger Toule
Edwᵃ Witheredge
Tymo. Prout
Geo. Spere
Symon Bird
Hen. Powning
Thom. Webster
Rob't Gowing
John Lake
Thom. Trot
John ffrench
Rich. Haule
Nicho. Boulton
Henry Gunlithe
Natha. Partridge
Thom. Dyer
Edwᵃ Wilder
Jos. Phippen
John Blake
Jasper Rush
John Gay
Rich. Goard
John Smeedly
Thom. ffox
Baptize Smeedly
Ste. Streete
John Maynard

Philip Tory
Rich'd Wooddy
Edmᵒ Shefeild
James Joanes
Tho. Chamb'lin
John Russell
Allen Conv'se
Lamb't Sutton
John Carter
James Parkʳ
     C. R., Vol. II. p. 53.

May, 1645.

Herb't Pelham
Joseph Hill
Mathewe Smith
Abraham Hawkins
Abra. Hackburne
Sam. ffellows
George Halsall
Abr. Parker
George Davies
Rich. Newberry
Natha. Bishop
John Stimson
Thom. Line
Antho. ffisher
Thom. Richards
Willi. Pardon
Thom. Holbrooke
George Allen
Willi. Davies
John Joanes   *stud.*
Sam. Stowe
Edwᵃ Jackson
Nicho. Wise
John Watson
Hugh Griffin
John Langford
Rich. Newton
John Toll
Jeremy More
Peetʳ Aspinwall
Edwᵃ Wyat
Rich. Leeds
James Umphryes
Rich. 'Blacke
James Nash
Benia. Thwinge
Samu. Davies
Rich. Bullock
Abr. Harding
Christo. Webbe
Thom. Barrill
John Morly
Henry Blacke
Edwᵃ Gilman
Lamb't Genery
John Gaye
Sam. Miles
John Daming

Ralph Day
Micha. Medcalfe
Sam. Sendall
Wm Hely
Hen. ffirnam
Thom. Roberts
Rob't Jenison
John Warren
Edw^a Devotion
Hen. Chamb'lin
Vincent Ruth
Thom. Barnes
Joseph Und'wood
Hen. Evance
John ffownell
Sam. Bright
Willi. Wenbane
John Bird
Harman Atwood
Natha. Greene
ffranc. Grissell
John Rydeat (78)
Wm. Parsons
Thom. Thacher
Rob't Longe
Thom. Reeves
Nicho. Chelett
Georg Dowdy
Hen. Aldridge
Willi. Patten
Eliiah Corlet (79)
C. R., Vol. II. pp. 78, 79.

6 May 1646.
Mathew Day
John Lewes
Nathani. Hadlock
John Hill
ffran. Heman
John Gingen
John Haynes
John Looker
Tho. Buckm'
Alex. Baker
Thom. Collier
Thom. Gardn'
Ben. Crispe
Wm. Pary
Wm. Dawes
Hen. Modsley
Joel Jenkins
Henry Thorpe
Geo. Woodward
Charles Sternes
John Wincoll
Willi. Duglas
Peter Place
John Collens
Rich. Everad
Josua Kent
Rob't Onion

Andrew Dewing
Antho. ffisher
Tho. Joanes
Isa. Walker
C. R., Vol. II. p. 124.
26 May 1647.
Ro. Chaulkly
James Green
Tho. Carter jr.
Mighil Smith
Manus Sally
James Pike
Rich'd Harrington
Sam. Carter
John Wayte
Law. Dowse
Wm. Bridges
Edw^a White
Mr. John Wilson
Wm. Harvy
Wm. Kerly
Rich. Newton
Thom. Tayer
John Nyles
John Stebben
John Whitny jr.
Moses Payne
David ffiske
David Stone
Philip Cooke
John Harris
Thom. Boyden
Mr. Samu. Danford
Willi. Ames
Dani. Kempster
Jonah Clooke
Thom. Huit
John Smith
Bartho. Cheever
John Miriam
ffranc. Kendall
Wm. Cotton
George Munioy
Rich. Hassall
Wm. Butrick
Geo. Barber
Ro. Wares
Thom. Jordan
John Metcalfe
John Bakor
Henry Wight
James Allen
Natha. Adams
Wm. Holbrooke
Thom. Dun
Thom. ffoster
Thom. Prat
Rob't Rendell
Tho. Poget
Geo. Davies

John Peirson
C. R., Vol. II. p. 163.
13 April 1648, at Springfield.
John Pynchon
Elitzur Holioak
Henry Burt
Roger Pritchard
Samu. Wright
Willi. Branch
C. R., Vol. II. p. 201.
10 May 1648.
Mr. Edw^a Denison
Georg Denison
Thom. Osburne
Benia. Negus
Thom. Hartshorn
Thom. Kendall
Wm. Hooper
Edw^a Tayler
Rich. Holbrooke
Willi. Daniel
Rich. Hardier
Wm. Needam
Samu. Basse
John Chickly
James Pemberton
Philem. Whale
Henry Rice
Mr. Samu. Danforth
Mr. Sam. Mather
Alex. Adams
John Staple
Benia. Negus
Henry Allen
John Peerce
Symon Tomson
Bartho. Porsune
C. R., Vol. II. p. 202.
5 April 1649.
Made free at Springfield.
Thom. Cooper
Griffin Jones
David Chapin
C. R., Vol. II. p. 227.
2 May 1649.
Mr. Willi. Browne
Joseph ffarnworth
Rob't Brick
John Maynard
Alexand' ffeild
Jona. Michell
Samu. Haward
Rob't Browne
Garret Church
Josua Stubbs
John Butler
John Turner
Thom. Saretell

Samu. Hides
Thom. Baker (227)
Josua ffisher
Corneli. ffisher
John Blanchard
John Hull
John Harwood
Will. Merriam
Nathani. Sternes
Peter Lyon (228)
C. R., Vol. II. pp. 227, 228.
3 May 1649.
John Ward
C. R., Vol. II. p. 228.
22 May 1650.
John Shepheard
Henry Prentice
Abraham Busby
Jacob Greene
Richard Stower
Thomas Welch
Wm. Pajne
David Mattocke
John Saunders
Robt Parmiter
Peeter Addams
John Jones
Joshua Edmonds
Wm. Underwood
Nathaniell Bale
Joseph Mirriam
Isacck Addington
Habbacuck Glover
Samuell foster
John Weld
Robt Harris
George Brand
Samuell Williams
Thomas Hanford
John Parker
Mr. John Knoules
John Ball
Rob' Pearse
Henry Mason
Wm. Ireland
Edmond Browne
C. R., Vol. IV. p. 1.
7 May 1651.
Mr. Sam. Haugh
Rich. Whitney
Rich. Ouldam
Wm. Hamlett
John Taylor
Henry Butler
George ffry
Wm. Pratt
Wm. Blake
Aron Way
Josias Convers

John Brookes
John Mousell
Hugh Thomas
Charles Grise
Martjn Saunders
Samuel Kingsly
Wm. Owen
David Walsby
Edward Rise
Solomon Johnson
Georg Dell
C. R., Vol. IV. p. 33.
26 May 1652.
Joseph Rocke — Bost.
James Richards — "
Tho. Emans — "
Henry Steevens — "
Jo. Marrjon — "
Rob'. Sanforth — "
Joshua Brooke — Conc.
Joseph Knight — Woob.
Hen. Baldwine — "
Rich. Gardiner — "
Jn° Sawen — Wate'
Ric. Norcrosse — "
Niccolas Willjams — Roxbur.
Isacke Heath — "
Wm. Garey — "
Peleg Heath — "
Tho. Brewar — "
Jacob ffrench — Weim.
Wm. Atwood — Charlst.
ffrancis Moore — "
Dan. Bloget — Camb.
Wm. Bordman — "
Solomon Martjn — And.
James Blake — Dorch.
Tho. Prentice — Rox.
Jn°. Pier Point — "
Moses Colljer — Hing.
Jn°. Fering — "
C. R., Vol. IV. p. 75.
Feb. 1652-3.
Tho. Wisewall — Dorch.
Norcross — Water.
Rob'. Howard — Dorch.
C. R., Vol. IV. p. 75.
18 May 1653.
Mr. Wm. Hubbard — I.
Symon Stone — W.
Sam. Stratten — "
Abra. Newell — Rox.
Jos. Griggs — "
Tho. Stowe — C.
Wm. Martjn — Read.
Wm. Eaton — "
Jonas Eaton — "
Tho. Marshall — "

Tho. Dwight — Ded.
Tho. Medcalfe — "
Wm. Hilton — Newb.
Tho. Skinner — Mald.
Jn°. Sprage — "
Nath. Upham — "
Rich. Boulter — Weim.
Tho. Whitman — "
Walter Cooke — "
Jn°. Guppee — "
Jn°. Thompson — "
Jonas Humphry — "
Richard Porter — "
Wm. Reade — "
Joshua Hubbard — Hing.
Jerremiah Hubbard — "
Jn°. Wight — Meadf.
Wm. Patridg — "
Joseph Clarke — "
Nath. Souther — Boston.
Steeven Pajne — "
Joseph Addams — "
C. R., Vol. IV. p. 113.
16 Nov. 1652.
Appeared before the Commissioners at Kittery, and submitted to the Government of Massachusetts; the record of their oath does not appear.
Tho. Withers
Jn°. Wincoll
Wm. Chadborn
Hugh Gunison
Tho. Spencer
Tho. Durston
Rob'. Mendam
Rise Thomas
James Emery
Christian Remeth
Niccolas ffrost
Rob'. Weimouth
Humphry Chadorne
Charles ffrost
Abraham Cunley
Richard Nason
Mary Bayly
Daniel Paule
Jn°. Diamont
Georg Leader
Jn°. Symons
Jn°. Greene
Hugbert Mattoone
Gowen Wilson
Wm. Palmer
Jerre. Shrires
Jn°. Hoord
Tho. Spinny
Nath. Lord

Joseph Mile
Antipas Mavericke
Niccolas Shapleigh
Antho. Emery
Reignald Jenkin
Jn°. White
Tho. Jones
Dennis Douning
Jn°. Andrewes
Daniell Davies
Phillip Babb
Wᵐ Everett

C. R., Vol. IV. p. 116.

22 Nov. 1652.

At Accomenticus or Gorgeana.

Mr. Edward Godfry
Tho. Crocket
Jn°. Alcocke
Wm. Dixon
Ricᵈ. Codogan
George Parker
Andrew Evered
Robᵗ. Knight
Wm. Rogers
Sam. Alcocke
Joseph Alcocke
Peter Wjer
Phillip Addams
Mr. ffrauncis Raines
     Lewis
Rob, Ed—— [blotted]
Phillip Hatch
Jn° Davis
Niccolas Bond
Mr. Edw. Johnson
Hugh Gajle
Wm. Garnesey
Rich. Banckes
Edw. Wentom
George Brancen
Mary Topp: acknowledged
  herself subject &c. only.
Mr. Wm. Hilton
Wm. Moore
Henry Donell
Edward Stirt
Rowland Young
Jn°. Parker
Arthur Bragdon
Wm. Ellingham
Jn°. Tuisdale jun'.
Tho. Courteous
Silvester Stover
Tho. Dennell
Mr. Edward Rushworth
Jn°. Harker
Niccolas Davis
Sampson Angier
Mr. Henry Norton

Robᵗ Hetherse
Wm. ffreathy
Jn° Davis
Jn° Tuisdall sen'.
Mr. Abra. Preble
Mr. Jn°. Couch
Mr. Tho. Whelewright
C. R., Vol. IV. p. 119.

4 July 1653.

Inhabitants of Wells: at
  Wells.
Joseph Emerson
Ezek. Knight
Jn°. Gooch
Joseph Boules
Jn°than Thing
John Barret sen'.
C. R., Vol. IV. p. 142.

5 July 1653. At Wells.
Henry Boade
Jn°. Wadly
Edmond Letlefeild
Jn°. Saunders
Jn°. White
Jn° Bush
Robᵗ Wadly
ffrauncis Litlefeild sen'.
Wm. Wardell
Samuell Austin
Wm. Hamans
Jn°. Wakefeild
Tho. Milles
Antho. Litlefeild
Jn°. Barrett juni.
Tho. Litlefeild
ffrauncis Litlefeild jun.
Nicho. Cole
Wm. Cole
C. R., Vol. IV. p. 142.

5 July 1653.
Inhabitants of Saco, sworn
  at Wells.
Thomas Willjams
Willjam Scadlocke
Christopher Hobbs
Thomas Reading
Richard Hitchcocke
James Gibbins
Thomas Rogers
Phillip Hinckson
Robert Booth
Richard Cowman
Ralfe Tristram
George Barlow
Jn°. West
Peter Hill
Henry Maddock

Thomas Hale
  C. R., Vol. IV. p. 145.

5 July 1653.

The Commissioners of Wells
  and Saco were empowered to give the oath of
  freemen to
John Smith   Saco.
Richard Ball   Wells.
Richard Moore   "
Jn°. Elson   "
Arthur Wormestall "
Edward Clarke   "
  C. R., Vol. IV. p. 145.

5 July 1653.

Inhabitants of Cape Porpus,
  sworn at Wells.
Morgan Howell
Christopher Spurrell
Thomas Warner
Griffin Mountague
John Baker
Wm. Renolls
Steven Batsons
Gregory Jeofferjes
Peter Turbat
Jn°. Cole
Symon Trott
Ambros Bury
  C. R., Vol. IV. p. 146.

8 May 1654.
John Morse
Jacob Eliott
Jn°. Tinker
Hugh Drury
Jn°. Parker
Tho. Weld
Jn°. Rugles
Nath. Glover
Isacke Jones
Tho. Hinksman
Sam. Hunt
Caleb Brooke
Tho. Marsh
Michaell Knight
Jn°. Kent
Tho. Battle
Tho. Herring
Joseph Child
ffranc. Whitmore
Tho. Sawer
Jn°. Greene
Joseph Champney
Alex. Marsh
Jn°. fasell
Edw. Addams
Wm. Chard
James Smith

Andrew ffoored
Jn°. Smith
Wm. Marble
   C. R., Vol. IV. p. 160.
   23 May 1655.*
Mr. Seaborn Cotton
Abra. Newell
Joseph Griggs
Tho. Stowe
Mr. Wm. Hubbard
Wm. Martyn
Wm. Eaton
Jonas Eaton
Thomas Marshall
Tim°. Dwight
Tho. Medcalfe
Wm. Hilton
Tho. Skinner
Jn°. Sprauge
Nathan. Upham
Rich. Boulter
Thomas Whitman
Walter Cooke
Jn°. Guppee
Jn° Thompson
Jonas Humphry
Rich. Porter
Wm. Reade
Symon Stone
Sam. St atten
Joshua Hubbard
Jerremy Hubbard
Jn°. Wight
Wm. Patridge
Joseph Clarke
Steeven Pajne
Joseph Addams
Wm. Johnson
   C. R., Vol. IV. p. 194.
   14 May, 1656.
Mr. Sam. Bradstreet
Mr. Sam. Whiting
Mr. Wm. Thompson
Job Lane
Jn°. Freary
Tho. Read
Tho. Basse
Hen. Wooddey
Abr. Jackewish
Jn°. Chadwicke
Steeven Gates
Abr. Ripley
Jn°. Ripley
   C. R., Vol. IV. p. 219.
   6 May 1657.
Willjam Lane
Henry Douglas

Joseph How
Wm. Dinsdale
Amiell Weekes
Roger Sumner
George Sumer
Justinian Houlden
Anthony Beers
Jer. Beales
Rich. Griffyn
Humphry Barrat
Jacob Park
Leonard Hurryman
Francis Weyman
Sam. Stone
Tho. ffaxon
Jn°. Dussett
   C. R., Vol. IV. p. 241.
   13 July 1658.
Inhabitants of Black Point, Blue Point, Spurwinke, and Casco Bay, sworn at Spurwinke, by Commissioners.
ffrancis Smaley
Nicho. White
Tho. Stamford
Jonas Bayly
Robert Corbyn
Nathaniell Wallis
Arthur Angur jun.
John Phillips
Rich. Martyn
Georg Lewis
Ambrose Boden
Samuell Oakeman
Andrew Brand
Mich. Madinde
Tho. Hamot
George Taylor
Henry Jocelyn
Georg Cleane
Rob' Jordan
Jn°. Bonighton
Richard ffoxwell
Henry Watts
ffranc. Neale
Abra. ffellew
Ambros Boden sen'.
Mich. Mitten
Jn°. Symes
Nico. Edgcomb
   C. R., Vol. IV. p. 295.
   30 May 1660.
Colonell Wm. Crowne
Augustine Lindon
Tho. Dwisdsall
Tho. Watkins

Hugh Clarke
Jn°. Majes
Sam. Majes
Jn° Elliott
Alex. Pannly
Wm. Wheeler
Jn°. Billing
Tho. Rice
Mathew Rice
Hen. Spring
Jacob Heurn
Nath Clap
Tho. Rand
Josiah Hubbard
James Whitton
John Nutting
Phillip Read
   C. R., Vol. IV. p. 336.
   27 May 1663.
Mr. Jn°. Croad
Charles Gott
Exercise Connant
Samuel Champneys
Jonathan Hide
Zech. Hicks
Abr. Holman
Jn°. Stratten
Rob' Harrington
Nath. Holland
Rob'. Twelves
Jn°. Ruggles
Jn°. Thirston
Wm. Clough
Nath. Hutchinson
Marke Batchiler
Dani. Pearse
Jos. Ellis
Wm. Toy
Laurenc. Waters
Tho. Collier
   C. R., Vol. IV. p. 416.
   19 Oct. 1664.
John Coldam Gloucester.
Mr. Robert Gibbs, Boston.
Mr. Abraham Browne "
Mr. Richard Price "
Arthur Mason "
Samuel Gallop "
   C. R., Vol. IV. p. 458.
   3 May 1665.
"The several persons underwrit returned by certificates from the several ministers and selectmen, were by public suffrage of both magistrates and Deputies admitted to

* Nearly a duplicate of the record under date of 18 May, 1653.

LIST OF FREEMEN.

3 May 1665.
"The several persons un-
derwrit returned by cer-
ti'cates from the several
ministers and selectmen,
were by public suffrage
of both Magistrates and
Deputies admitted to
freedom, and took their
oaths accordingly."
Capt. George Corwin Sal.
John Endecott "
Zerubbabl Endecott "
Eliazer Hauthorne "
John Corwin "
Wm. Browne jr. "
Jn°. Putman "
Joseph Porter "
Rich. Leech "
Sam. Eburne sen. "
Jn°. Rucke "
James Browne "
Phillip Cromwell "
Rich. Hollingsworth "
Edw. Humber "
Joshua Rea "
Xtopher Babridge "
Georg May Bo.
Joseph Belknap "
Amos Richardson "
Tho. Joy "
Deane Winthrop "
Nath. Reynolds "
Benj. Thirston "
John Toppan "
ffrancis Bacon "
Nath. Greene "
Humphry Davy "
James Alljn "
Abijah Savage "
Henry Taylor "
Tho. Underwood "
Wm. Hazzey "
Benj. Muzzey "
Tho. Hoole "
Hen. Messenger "
Jn°. Minot Dor.
James Minot "
Stephen Minot "
Dani. Preston "
David Jones "
Wm. Weekes "
Edw. Blake "

Jn°. Blackman Dor.
Jn°. Lewis Lanc.
Georg Colton Spr.
Edm°. Quinsey Br.
Isak Sternes Wat
Jn°. Stone "
Steven Willoues Camb.
Jn°. Marret "
Georg Cooke "
James Trowbridge "
Jn°. Grout "
Joseph Esterbrooke "
Nath. Saltonstal Hav.
Edmo. Chamberlaine
Chelm.
Jn°. Wright "
Jn°. Stevens "
Jno Martin (463) "
James Heildrick "
Herlakenden Symons Gloc.
Sam. Ward Marbh.
Stephen Pajne Mald.
Peter Tuffs "
Rich. Cutts Port.
Jn°. Gold "
Tho. Baker "
Shubal Dumer Newb.
Tho. Steevens Sudb.
Ri. Meade Rox.
Edm°. Eddenden "
Tho. Eames (464) "
C. R., Vol. IV. pp. 463, 464.
3 May, 1665.
Mr. Phillip Nelson Rowley
Tho. Nelson "
Jn°. Trumble "
Benj°. Scott "
. C. R., IV. p. 465.
11 Oct. 1665.
Thomas Merrick Springf".
C. R., IV. p. 557.
23 May 1666.
Mr. Joseph Cooke Camb.
Daniel Wellow "
Jn°. Swayne "
Jn°. Addams "
Tho. Browne "
Tho. Phelabrowne "
Tho. Cheney "
James Hubbard "
Rob't Ayer Haver.
Tho. Ayer "

Peter Ayer Haver.
Tho. Whittier "
James Davis "
Jn°. Dow "
Tho. Lillford "
Sam. Converse Wob.
Jn°. Benjamin Wat".
Edw. Allen Bost.
Jno. Bracket "
Joseph Davis "
Seth Perry "
Tho. ffitch "
Sam. Norden "
Georg Mang "
Edm°. Eddington "
Tho. Matson jun. "
Jn°. Batchelor Red.
Edw. Burns Hng.
Ben. Bosworth "
Jn°. Cole sen'. Had.
Joseph Balduin "
franc. Bernard "
Phillip Russell "
James Bapson Glo.
Wm. Kerly Marl.
Edm°. Gate Sal.
Sam. Moody Newb.
Caleb Moody "
Isack Butter Med.
Nicho. Rocket "
Benja. Gibbs Bost.
Abr. Willjams Marlb.
Nath. Weare Hampt.
Hen. Page "
Rob't Vose Milt.
Antho. Gullifer "
Nicho. George sen'. Dorch.
Obadiah Hawes "
Jn°. Capen jun. "
Tho. Peirse "
Rob't Spurr "
Timo. Tileston "
Jn°. Gill "
Tho. Smist jun. "
Ezra Clap "
Wm Cheny Rox.
Jn°. Moore "
Tho. ffoster "
Wm Lyon "
Jn°. Kingman Wey".
Sam. Pratt "
Sam. White "
Jn°. Vining "

Column 1

Name	Place
Tho. Bayly	Wey^m.
James Nash	"
Jacob Nash	"
Laurenc Hamond	Bost.
Robt. Coxe	"
Hugh Amos	"
Moses ffiske	Dov^r.
Peter Coffyn	"
Jn°. Woodman	"
Jn°. Davis	"
Jn°. Martjn	"
Antho. Nutter	"
Tho. Roberts	"
Tobias Davis	"
Tho. Eaton	Hav.
Jn°. Johnson	"
Jn°. White	——
Elish. Huthinson	
David Saywell	
Eph. Turner	
Jn°. Turner	
Caleb Watson	
Jn°. Crow	
Jn°. Browne	
Jn°. Samborne	Hampton
Nath. Batchelor	"
Wm. Marston	"
Hen. Dow	"

C. R., Vol. IV. p. 562.

29 April 1668.

Name	Place
Mr. James Russell	Charlstown
Jn°. Heyman	"
Nathani Rand	"
Peter ffrothrington	"
Jn°. Louden	"
Jn° Benjamin	Wat'town.
Nath. Coolidge	"
Jonath. Whitney	"
Jonatha. Browne	"
Symon Stacy	Ipswich
Jn°. Whiple	"
Tho. West	Salem
Henry West	"
Samuell Archard	"
Jn°. Massey	"
Wm. Downton	"
Jn°. Ingersoll	"
Jn°. Pease	"
Jn°. Dodge sen^r.	Bass River
Nath. Stone	"
Peter Woodbury	"
Ephrajm Hereck	"
Wm. Peelsbury	Newbery.
James Ordaway	"
Nath. Clarke	"
Tristram Coffin	"
Henry Leonard	Lynn

Column 2

Name	Place
Nehemiah Jewet	Lynn
Tho. Call jun.	Malden
James Nicholls	"
Tho. Hall	Cambridge.
Tho. Philebrowne	"
Jn°. Swan	"
Nath. Handcock	"
Sam. Hastings	"
Jn°. Addams	"
Thom. Browne	"
Nath. Smith	Haverill
Steven Dow	"
Robert Emerson	"
Ralph Holton	Lancs^r
Henry Kelly	"
James ffowle	Wooborne
Benj. Bullard	Meadfeild
Sam. Gary	Rocksbury
Tho. Philbrick	Hampton
Sam. Wadsworth	Milton
Sam. Smith	North Hampton.
Jn°. ffarrington	Dedham

C. R., Vol. IV. p. 600.

24 Oct. 1668.

Name	Place
Jn° Green	Maulden
Wm Greene	"
Symon Crosbee	Billirrikey.
Thomas Day	Springfeild

C. R., Vol. IV. p. 624.

19 May 1669.

" Persons admitted to ffreedom by this Court, and those that tooke their oaths are set down first; those that tooke it not are under the line."

Mr. Tho. Deane
James Whetcombe
Daniel Turill
Sam. Norden
Jn°. Mosse
Joseph Parsons
Jn°. Gidney
Barthol. Gidney
Sam. Cheevers
Jn°. Pickering
Joseph Grafton
———
Mr. Jn°. Davenport sen^r.
Mr. Jn°. Shearman
Mr. Sam. Torrey
Mr. Rich. Hubbard
James How
Mr. Jn°. Davenport jun.
Jn°. Prescott
Rich. Wheeler
Jn°. Moor

Column 3

Jn°. Rugg
Jno°. fletcher
Joakim Harvey
Tho. Daniel
Wm Vauhan
Rich. Cumings
Henry Deering
Jn°than Wade jun.
Jn°. Conney — sworn July
Moses Bradford
Sam Mason
Jn°. Roberts
Jn°. Gorton
James Kent — Newb.
Jn° Kent
Jn°. Bartlet jun.
Jn°. Wells
Abiel Somersby
Henry Jacquish
Benja. Lowell
John Bayley
Sam. Perly
Nehemiah Abbot
Georg Lyon
Ezra Clap
Ebenezar Clap
Tho. Gunn
James Cornish
Jn°. Roote
Tho. ffarnum
Jn°. Steephens
Jn°. fry
Steven Osgood
Georg Abbat
Wm. Chandler — And.
Andrew ffoster
Jn°. Maxwell
Laurenc. Willis
Wm. Greenough
Benj Gage
Jn°. Bayly — Newb.
Nath. Hancock
Jn°. Bayley — Rowley
Mathew Edwards
Jn°. Keepe — Spr.
Isack Graves — sworn
Henry Jacquish
Benj. Kelly
Jn°. Hastings
Boaz Browne
Ezek. Jewet
Antho. Austin
Jn°. Kelly
Benja. Rolfe
Thomas Wiggin

C. R., Vol. IV. p. 629.

11 May 1670.

Mr. Jn°. Chickering — Chars.
Daniel Edmonds — "

Name	Place
Tho. White	Chars.
Abraham Smith	"
Sam. Peirce	"
Joseph ffrost	"
Tho. Chadwell	"
Sollomon Phipps jun.	"
Joseph Ketle	"
Sam. Ketle	"
Wm. Symonds	Woo.
Roger Kenicot	"
Tho. Green	"
Jn°. Baldin	Bill.
Samuell Maning	"
Jn° Bracket	"
Mr. Jn° Oxenbridge	Bost.
Henry Tompson	"
Adam Niccolls	"
Mr. Sam. Willard	Groton
Wm. Lakin	"
Mathyas farnworth	"
Tho. Patch	"
Henry Bayly	Bev'ly
John Black	"
John Gally	"
Jn°. Woodbery	"
Tho. West	"
Mr. Beter Bulkley	Conc.
John Haywood	"
Thomas Mason	
	North Hamp'.
Tho. Bascome	"
Wm. Webster	Hadley
Joseph Baldwin	"
Joseph Plumer	Newb.
Benj. Rolfe	"
John Poore jun.	"
ffranc. Thurlo	"
Nicho. Batt	"
Job Pilsbury	"
John Gerrish	Dov.
Wm. Bartol	Marbhd.
Benja. Leeds	Dorc.
Henry Haggit	
Dani. Gott	
Wm. Rayner	
Jn°. Batchiler	
Wᵐ ffiske	
John Albye	

C. R., Vol. IV. p. 651.

11 Oct. 1670.

John Sandford
John Gipson
John Warren
David Cop
Samuel Worcester
Nicholas Wallington

C. R., Vol. IV. p. 660.

31 May 1671.

Name	Place
Giles fyfield	Charls.

Name	Place
Ric. Asting	Charls.
Tho. Hale	"
Nath. ffrothingham	"
Joseph Lynd	"
Abr. Smith	"
John Call	"
Sam, ffrothingham	"
Mr. Alexand' Nowell	"
Tho. Parkes	Cambr.
Jn°. Tuttle	Lyn
Mr. Josiah flynt	Dorch.
Antho. Newton	"
Hen. Leadbetter	"
Robt. Spurr	"
James Convers	Wob.
Eljazer Jaco	"
Mr. Wm. Brinsmead	
Hen. Collins jun.	
Allin Broad	
Jn°. Penniman	Brant.
Moses Belcher	"
Caleb Hubard	Hing.
Josh. Lyncoln	"
Joseph Baldwin	Hadl.
Noah Coleman	"
ffr. Wainewright	Ips.
Wm. White	"
Isack ffoster	"
Sam. Younglove	"
Rich Waker	"
Wm. Story jun.	"
Arthur Abbot jun.	"
Robt. Allin	Dedh.
Jn°. Richards	"
Nath. Heaton	"
Jn°than ffuller	"
Medad Pumrey	North Hamp.
Jn°. Barber	"
Charls fferry	Spring.
Jn°. Riley	"
Tho. Hobbs	Topsf.
Paul White	Newb.
Tho. Noyes	"
Jn°than Morse	"
James Smith	"
John Smith	"
John Knight jun.	"
Isack Phelps	Westf.
Joseph Whiting	—
Jonothan Corwin	Salem.
Jn°. Marston	"
Eliaz'. Gidney	"
Jn°. Maskor	"
Tho. Ingolls (676)	"
Jn°. Alden 3d Chh.	Boston.
ffranc. Robinson	"
Jn°. Mellowes	"
Jonathan Jackson	"
Wm. Hoare	"

Name	Place
James Hill 3ᵈ Chh.	Boston.
Jn°. Marshall	"
Ambrose Daws	"
Ezra Morse	"
Jn°. Lytlefeild	Ded.
Jn°. Holton	"
Sam. How	Sud.
Jn°. Roberts 1ˢᵗ. Ch.	Bosto[n]
Edmo. Ranger	"
Bartho. Toppn	"
Jn°. Temple	"
Jn°. farnham	"
Jn°. Moore	"
Jn°. Cotte	"
Jn°. Cleanesby	"
Robᵗ. Wᵐs	"
Tho. Overmore	"
Mr. Jn°. Saffyn	"
Capt. Tho. Lake	"
Josh. Holdsworth	"
Jn°. Barnard	Watʳ.
Sam. Livermore	"
Jn°. Bright	"
Sam. Craft	Rox.
Ephraim Hunt	Wey.
Jn°. Rogers	"
Benj. Gage	Havʳ.
Sam. Gage	"
Rogʳ Kennicot	Mald.
Sam. Lee	"
Tho. Green	"
Tho. Burnham jun.	Ips.
Tho. Beard	"
Jn°. Bickford sen.	Dorch.
Robᵗ Burnm	"
James Coffyn	—
Tho. Bill (677)	Hamp.

C. R., Vol. IV. pp. 676, 677.

15 May 1672.

Name	Place
Mr. Urian Oakes	Camb.
Mr. Joseph Dudley	Roxbu.
Wm. Laking	Groaton
Mathias farnworth	"
Jn°. Morse	"
Joseph Morse	"
Nath. Lawrence	"
Jn°thª Sautell	"
Jn°thª Morse	"
Mr. Jn° Winslow	Boston
Dani. Henchman	"
Ephraim Savage	"
Joseph Wheeler	"
Mannasseth Brike	"
Symon Amery	"
Tim° Thornton	"
Hen. Allin	"
Edw. Grant	"
James Townsend	"

		8 Oct. 1672.		Mr. Thomas Graves	Ch.
Wm. Smith	Boston.			Mr. Joseph Browne	——
Sam. Bridge (688)	"	Mr. Solomon Stoddard		Mr. Sam. Brakenbury	Ch.
Wm. Griggs	"		North Ham.	Humphry Bradshaw	Camb.
Ephraim Searl	"	George Lane	Hing.	Samuell Oldam	"
Abell Porter jun.	"	Dr. Leornard Hoare	Bost.	Nath. Robbinson (718)	"
Isack Brookes	Woob.	Tho. Lull	Ips.	Wm Davis	Rox.
Joseph Richardson	"	Sam. Wight	Medf.	James Day	Ips.
Wm Ellery	Gloc.	Eph. Wight	"	Mr. Joseph Gerrish	New.
Tho. Pinney	"	Joseph Croufot	Springf.	Jno Bailey	Wey.
Georg Laines	Ports.	Henry Walker	Glocest.	ffrancis Browne	"
Jno Breuster	"	*C. R., Vol. IV. p.* 705.		Elisha Elzie	Newb.
Robt Purrington	"	7 May 1673.		James Bayly	"
Rich. Shortridg	"	Mr. Peter Lydget		Dani. Cheny	"
Jno. Dennet	"		1a. Ch. Bost.	Joshua Browne	"
Jno. Thompson	"	Mr. Samuel Shrimpton	"	Sam. Poore	"
Tho. Eggerly	Dovr.	Mr. Elisha Cooke	"	Moses Pilsbury	"
Jno. Rand	"	Mr. Eljakim Hutchinson	"	Benja. Morse	"
Jno. Dam	"	Mr. John Usher	"	Sam. Bartlet	"
Stev. Jones	"	Mr. Jno ffaireweather	"	Hen. Ingalls	And.
Jno Wingat	"	Mr. John Clarke	"	Jno. Lovejoy	"
Thos. Layton	"	Mr. Isack Addington	"	John Barker	"
Tho. Ollivr	Cambr.	Mr. John Buttolph	"	John Baker	Drch.
Natha. ffiske	"	Samuel Bridge	"	Ellis Wood	"
Jno Morse	Watr.	Mr. Xtopher Clarke	"	Edw. West	"
Wm Torrey	Weym.		3d Ch. Bost.	Jos. Heyward	Conc.
Micajah Torrey	"	Mr. John Joyliffe	"	Nathan. Billings	"
Joseph Prat	"	Mr. Edward Willis	"	Abra. Bryant	Red.
Ric. Temple	Conc.	Mr. Nathaniel Daven-		Mr. Gershom Hobbart	
Tho. Deane	"	port	"		Hing.
Gershom Brooks	"	Tho. Bingley	"	James Bate	"
Obadiah Morse	Medf.	Paul Batt	"	Clement Bate	"
Jnothn Morse	"	Timothy Batt	"	Mr. Zecha. Whitman	Hull
Joseph Morse	"	Mr. John Woodmansey	"	Benj. Bosworth	"
Nath. Whiting	"	John Drury	"	Tho. Loring	"
Ezekiel Jewet	Rowley	James Bracket	"	Jno. Loring	"
Abr. Haseltine	"	Mr. Edw. Willis	"	Jno. Lobdell	"
Tho. Rimgton	"	Mr. Jno. Walley, mercht	"	Isack Lobdell	"
Jno. Watson	"	Lyonel Wheately	"	Benj. Loring	"
Jnoth. ffuller	Dedh.	Robert Mason	"	Sampson Shoare	"
Edw. West	Medfie.	John Walley, mariner	"	Abra. Jones	"
Mr. Hope Atherton		Mr. John Pole	"	Jno Cumins	Tops.
	Hatfeid.	Rich. Paddeshall	"	Isa. Cumins	"
Jno Coleman	"	John Wilkins	"	Isack Easty	"
Thadeus Riddan	Lyn	John Osborne	2d Ch. Bo.	Jno Row	Glo.
Josep Gardiner	Salem	Hopestil foster	"	Nathan. Joseljn	Lanc.
Rich. Hutton	Wenh.	ffrancis Hudson	"	Sam. Belden	Hatf.
Joseph Rice	Marlb.	Wm. Greenore jun.	"	Dani. Warner	"
Tho. Chubbuck		Math. Barnard	"	Wm. Gull	"
Tho. Lincolne		Daniel Travis	"	Chileab Smith	Hadl.
Jno Beale		Rich. Bennet	"	Jos. Warner	"
Dani. Cushin		Capt. Sam. Scarlet	"	Jno Tucker	Ports.
Mathias Bridges		John Anderson senr.	"	Nicho. Woodbery	Bevrly
Joseph Bate		Joseph Cooke	"	Peter Noyce	Sudb.
Benj. Bate		Obadiah Swift	Dorch.	John Goodenow	"
Samuell Bate		John Bird	"	Tho. Barnes	Marlb.
Wm. Hearsy		Eliazr Hawes	"	James Vales	Medf.
Onesepherus Marsh		Joseph Weekes	"	Mr. Charls Nicholate (719)	
Jacob Beale		Samuel Topliffe	"		Salem
Caleb Beale (689)		Jno Wthrington	"	*C. R., Vol. IV. pp.* 718, 719.	
C. R., Vol. IV. pp. 688, 689.					

15 Oct. 1673.

Nathaniel Peirce   B. 1 Ch.
Mathew Atkins   B. 2ᵈ Ch.
Boaz Browne   Conc.
Epbraim Clarke   Medf.
Wm. Coleman   Glo.
Stephen Cooke   Mendˢ
Danel Lovet   "
Abra. Staple   "
Joseph Steevens   "
Samuel Read   "
Hope Tyler   "
    C. R., Vol. IV. p. 732.

20 Dec. 1673.

John Lovejoy
John Barker
Henry Ingalls
    C. R., Vol. IV. p. 737.

9 January 1673–4.

Jnᵒ Noyes   New.
Cutting Noyes   "
John Lunt   "
Abra. Addams   "
John Badger   "
Joseph Gerrish   "
Nathaniel Brewer   Rox.
Mr. Wᵐ Addams   Ded.
Sam. Capen   Dorchᵗ.
    C. R., Vol. IV. p. 737.

11 March 1673–4.

Pen Townsend   B.
Mr. John Rodgers   Ips.
Mr. Samuel Cobbet   "
Robᵗ. Kinsman   "
Thomas Clarke   "
Daniell Hovey   "
Abraham ffitt   "
Joseph Goodhue   "
Joseph Whiple   "
Philemon Dane   "
Tho. ffisher   Ded.
Joseph Pratt   Weym.
Tho. Andrew   Hing.
Nath. Cutler   Ch.
James Bacon   Roxb.
Josias Richardson
         Chelmsfo.
Eliazer Browne   "
Jacob Warren   "
    C. R., Vol. IV. p. 738.

27 May 1674.

Mr. Daniel Epps   Ips.
Tho. Jacob   "
Tho. Metcalf   "
Nico. Wallis   "
Nathaniel Addams   "

Nathan: Rust   Ips.
Tho. ffrench   "
Jnᵒ Lumpson
Jnᵒ Pebody
Joseph farnum
Jnᵒ. Rugles senʳ.
Elnathan Chancy [Cambᵗ.]
Ruben Luxford   "
Andrew Boardman   "
Jnᵒ. Jackson   "
Daniel Markham   "
Jnᵒ Buss
Jacob french
Wm Seavir
Obadiah Morse
Tho. Harvie
Antho. Ellings
Richard Sampson
Abell Poster
Caleb Pumbrey   N. Hamp.
Ebenezer White   Weym.
Edw. Addams   Med.
Joseph Wright   "
Gershom flagg   "
Samuel Walker   Woob.
James Thompson   "
Israel Walker   "
Jnᵒ Snow   "
    C. R., Vol. V. p. 1.

7 Oct. 1674.

Samuel Douse   Ch.
Tho. Bligh   Bost.
Rich. Sharpe   "
Tho. Smith
Wᵐ Ingram
Dudley Bradstreet
    C. R., Vol. V. p. 15.

22 July 1674.

At a Court at Pemaquid the
   following named persons
   took the oath of fidelity.

Thomas Humphreys
Robert Gamon
Willjam Waters
John Dolling
Thomas Cox
Robᵗ Edmunds
Ambrose Hanwell
John Wriford
Eljas Trick
John Pride
George Bickford
Reynald Kelley
Jnᵒ̣ Cole
Capt. Edmnd Pattestall
Mr. Ichabod Wisewall
Mr. Richard Olliver
Wm. Buckford

Edward Barton
Richᵈ. Hill
Henry Curtis
francis Browne   Tops.
Richᵈ. Warren   1 Ch.
Henry Stoakes   Rox.
Wm. Denlo
Edwᵈ. Dorr
Jnᵒ Dare
Geor. Burnet
Nicho. Osbourne
Tho. Parker   Conc.
David Olliver   Billᵗ.
Emanuel Whichalls   Ports.
Jnᵒ Cock
Tho. Phillips
Tho. Hilman
Nicco. Carary
Jnᵒ Parker
Nicco. Deming
Abell Hoggeridge
Edward Cole
Jnᵒ WildGoose
Tho. Parnell
Aaron Beard
Gregory Langberry
Abra. Clarke
Tho. Cox jun.
Henry Curtis jun.
Shadrick Cox
Richard Cox
Richard Pearce jun.
Robert Cauly
Tho. Adger
Richard Bradeway
Richard Bucknell
Wm. Edwards
Tho. Cox
Wm. Waters
Wm. Welcome
Jnᵒ. Bessell
Peter Collins
Richard Glass
Tho. Phillips
Henry Palmer
Jnᵒ Palmer jun.
Phillip Bry
Wm. Phillips
Jnᵒ. Stover
Jnᵒ. Palmer senʳ.
Robrt Edmnds
James Widger
Tho. Harls
Jnᵒ Gingden
Nico. Vallack
Jnᵒ Selman
Wm. Trout
Nico. Heale
Georg Bucknell
Wm. Cox

Tho. Cox
  C. R., Vol. V. p. 17.
  12 May 1675.
John Valentine   Bost.
Joseph Webb   "
Elisha Audljn   "
Sam. Ware   "
Jn°thª Bridgham   "
Peircy Clarke   "
John Davis   "
Joshua Gee   "
Benja. Dyer   "
Edw. Thwing
Sam. Gardiner   Salem
Samuel Warner   Ips.
Tho. Weld   "
Tho. Gittings   "
Symon Chapman   "
Nath. Warner   "
James Bracket   Bev.
Andrew Boardman   Camb.
Ruben Luxford   "
Dani. Markeham   "
John Jackson   "
Ebenez' Wiswall   "
  C. R., Vol. V. p. 25.
  21 Feb. 1675–6.
Jn° Tucker   3ᵈ Bost.
Jn° Noyes   "
Natha. Willjams   "
Dani. Gookin jun.   Camb.
Jn° Pike   Salis.
Hen. Trow   Ips.
Jn°. Jewet   "
Rob' Pierpoint   "
Jn° Atwood   Bost. 2ᵈ
Joseph Knight   Woo.
Georg Abbot   And.
Xtopher Osgood   "
Tho. Osgood   "
Jacob french   Bille.
Tho. Russell   Charles.
Jn° Clifford   Hamp.
Joseph Barret   Chelms.
[illegible] Amistreale   ——
Tho. Dyer   Weym
  C. R., Vol. V. p. 70.
  3 May 1676.
Mr. Sam. Alcock   Boston
Mr. Dani. Russell   Charl.
Zech. Johnson   "
Isaack ffowle   "
Zech. fferris   "
John Goodwin   "
Timo. Baker   Northam.
Joseph Person   "
Jn° Bridgman   "

Judah Wright   Northam.
Sam. Smith   "
Mr. Jn° Younglove   Hadly
Samuel Wentworth   Dov.
  C. R., Vol. V. p. 73.
  11 Oct. 1676.
Richard Hall   Bradf.
Dani. Hazeltine   "
Jn° Hardy   "
Jn° Hubbard   Ips.
Jn° Jewet   "
Benja. Emons   Bo. 3ᵈ Ch.
Sam. Davis   Northam.
Nehemia Allin   "
Jn° Knight   "
Jn° Dowse   Charls.
  C. R., Vol. V. p. 112.
  23 May 1677.
Mr. Jn° Price   Salem
Jn° Higinson jun.   "
Jn° Hauthorne   "
Manasses Marston   "
Henry Kirrey   "
Mr. Sam. Nowel   Charls.
Jn° Phillips   "
Xtopher Goodin   "
James Millar   "
Jn° Blany   "
W'm. Gibson   Boston 1 Ch.
Nathani Barnes   "
Edwᵈ Ashley   "
Jn° Cadwell   Ips.
Jn° Wales   Dorch.
James Blake   "
Joseph Roads   Lin.
Jn° White   Rox.
Jabez ffox   Camb.
Jn° Rogers   Wey.
Jn° Bayly   "
Nathani. Gay   Dedh.
Tho. Aldridge   "
Nath. Kingsbery   "
Jn° Weare   "
Wm. Avery   "
Jn° Hollioke   Spr.
Sam. Stoddar   Hingh.
Andrew Lane   "
Jn° Tucker   "
Richᵈ Dumer jun.   Newb.
Hen. Short   "
Steph. Greenleaf   "
Jacob Toppan   "
Rich. Bartlet jun.   "
Tho. Pearly   "
Wm. ffoster   Rowley
Nath. Barker   "
Obadiah Morse   Meadf.
Edwᵈ Addams   "

Eljaz' Addams   Meadf.
Jn°th Morse   "
Jos. Bullin   "
Jn° Walker   Wooburn
Jn° Carter   "
Jn° Brarboun   "
franc. fletcher   Concord
Timo. Wheeler   "
Jn° Merriam   "
Sam. Jones   "
Sam. Lampson   Redding
Jn° Eaton   "
Henry Merrow   "
Sebred Taylor   "
  C. R., Vol. V. p. 126.
  10 Oct. 1677.
John Clarke   B. 3 C.
Gilbert Cole   "
Robert Butcher   ——
Nathaniel Patten
Jn° Wales sen'.   Dor.
Sam. Hix   "
Henry Withengton   "
Amos Woodward   Camb.
Dani. Champney   "
John Wells   Rox.
Tho. Pierce   Woob.
Jn° Smeadley   Conc.
Joseph Boynton   Row.
Alexand' Sessions   And.
Benja. Lincolne   Hing.
John Chubbuck   "
John fering   "
Tho. Gill jun.   "
  C. R., Vol. V. p. 146.
  8 May 1678.
Joseph Bridgham
  1 Ch. Bost.
Joshua Windsor   2 Ch.
Jonas Clarke   "
Hen. Dauson   "
Wm Way   "
Jn° Barnard   "
Tho. Bark'   "
Jn° Goffe   "
Wm. Sumer   "
Mr. Peter Thatcher   3 Ch.
Mr. Sam. Seawall   "
Mr. Elnath. Chancey   Camb.
Timo. Lyndall   Salem
Isack ffoot   "
Roger Hill   "
Wm. Barker   "
Edw. Read   "
Benj. Parmiter   "
Richard Riff   "
Francis Girdler   "
Jn° Mascoll   "
Walter Cloys   "

Joseph fairbank	Ded.
Tho. ffisher	"
Sam. Guile	"
Benj. Miles	"
Joseph Wight	"
Josia ffisher	"
Rob't Weare	Hamp.
Jonath. ffreeman	"
Jnº. Clifford	"
Wm. ffuller	"
Jnº Parker	Mauld.
Joseph Lynds	"
Dani. Thirston	Meadf.
Sam. Baker	Hull
Joseph Benson	"
Samuel Prince	"
Jnºth. Vickree	"
Tho. Toleman	Dorch.
Jnº. Toleman	"
Nath. Glover	"
James ffoster	"
Incre. Sumer	"
Hope Clap	"
Jnº Baker	"
Wm. Ryall	"
Josia Chapen	Brant.
Jos. Peniman	"
Sam. Penniman	"
Jos. Parmiter	"
Steph. Payne jun.	"
Jnº Lazell	Hing.
Sam. Thaxter	"
Tho. Marsh	"
Jos. Walker	Biller.
Tho. Patten	"
Sam. ffrost	"
Obadia Perry	"
Mr. Edw. Taylor	Westf.
Jnº Maudsley	"
Vickry Sike	Spr.
Isa. Cakebread	"
Luke Hitchcoke	"
Jnº Richardson	Woob.
Tho. Bankroft	Red.
Jnº Townsend	"
Rich. Phillips	Weym.
Sam. Humphry	"
Joseph Dyar	"
Edmo. Grover	Bevʸ.
Nehem. Grover	"
Isa. Woodbery	"
Hump. Woodbery	"
Rob'. Bradbuth	"
Ric. Patch	"
Jnº Blatt	"
Jnº Richᵈˢ.	"
Jnº Patch	"
Tho. Holman	Milton
Ephr. Tucker	"
Manasses Tucker	"
Timo. Nash	Hadl.

Tho. Hale	Hadl.
Jnº Russell	"

C. R., Vol. V. p. 175.

2 Oct. 1678.

Mr. Isack ffoster	Charls.
Jnº Pengilley	Ips.
Enock Hubbard	Hing.
Sam. Man	Ded.
Jnº Brewer	Sud.
Jonas Prescot	"
Tho. Reade jun.	"
Wm. Addams	"
Joseph ffreeman	"
Samˡˡ Carter	Woob.
Jnº Kendall	"
Jos. Winge	"
John Lynds	Mald
Jnº Greenland	"

C. R., Vol. V. p. 202.

15 Oct. 1679.

Mr. John Browne	Red.
Benja. ffitch	"
Hananiah Parker	"
Nath. Gooding	"
Peter Tuffes	Mald.
francis Jones	"
Mathew Cushin jun.	Hing.
Jnº Smith jun.	"
Dani. Cushin	"
Josia Levet	"
Joseph Wing	Wo.
Joseph Lyon	Rox.
Jnº Dole	New.
Sam. Butterick	Conc.
Jnº Prescot	"
Ephraim Winship	Camb.
Jnº Marrion	"

C. R., Vol. V. p. 232.

4 Feb. 1679–80.

" Ordered, that the Honᵇˡᵉ Georg Russell Esq., now resident with us in Boston, be admitted to the freedom of this corporation, if he please to accept thereof." Marg. note. " He accepted it, and took his oath 13 ffeb. 79, before the Governor and Assistants."

C. R. Vol. V. p. 259.

19 May 1680.

Mr. Jnº Bowles	Rox.
Mr. Edw. Pason	"
Jnº. Grafton	Salem
Resolved White	"
Benja. Thwing	1 C. Bost.
Jerr. Dumer	"

Jnº Thing	1 C. Bost.
Jacob Hurd	"
Tho. Chard	"
Jnº Cotton	2ᵈ Ch.
Cotton Mather	"
Wm. Coleman	"
Jabez Broune	Sud.
Jnº Held	Chelmsf.
Eliaʳ Ball	"
Jonathan Tyng	"
Mr. Jose. Hawley	North.
Davjd Burt	"
Wm. Smead	"
Jnº. Woodward	"
Jonathan Hunt	"
Joshua Pomrey	"
Eliazʳ frary	"
Joseph Dodge	Bevʳ.
Jnº Balch	"
Paul Thorndick	"
Richᵈ. Norman	Marblehᵈ
Jnº Legg	"
Nathan. Walton	"
Richᵈ Mounteque	"
Mr. Tho. Shephard	Charls.
Mr. Neh. Hubbard	
	Camb. Villᵗ.
Ebenezʳ Wiswall	" "
Sam. Robbins	" "
Jnº Gardiner	Wob.
Jnº Chadwick	"
Mr. Wiglesworth	Mald.
Peletiah Smith	"
Tho. Putnam jun.	
	[illegible.]
Wm. Stacy	
Zache Marsh	
Symon Booth	
Israel How	
Benj. Leeds	
John Pason	
Symon Willard	Ips.
Joseph Pitty	"
Nath Humphry	"
Abra. Whitman	Wey.
Wm. Pratt	"
Mr. Edw. Taylor	West.
David Ashley	"
Jeddedia Dewy	"
Sam. Roote	"
Joseph Pomry	"
Nath. Melby	Hull
Jnº. Hanchet	"
Benj. Bosworth	"
Abr. Jones	"
Rob' Gold	"
Jonathan Nile	"
Nathani. Bosworth	"
Sam. Prince	"
Zach. Hund	"
Jose. Bosworth	"

Iseck Vickrey	Hull
Steven Lincoln	Hingh.
Mr. Jer. Shep'd	Lynn
Tho. Layton	"
Ralph King	"
Rob'. ffuller	"
Jn° felton	"
Jos. Phippen	"
Mr. Dani'. D [blotted]	
Japhet Chapin	Spring.
Sam. Ely	"
Tho. Shelden	Biller.
C. R., Vol. V. p. 260.	

13 Oct. 1680.

Mr. Tho. Cheever	
	1 C. Bost.
Nicho. Willis	"
Mr. Deodat Lawson	3 C.
Sam. Ballard	Cha.
Mr. Edw. Pason	Rox.
Danie. Kellum jun.	Wenh.
John Knolton	"
Sam. Knolton	"
Tho. Bayly	"
Sam. Abby	"
Sam. ffiske	"
Tho. Prentice sen'.	
	Camb. Vill.
Tho. Prentice jun.	"
Tho. Parke sen'.	"
Jn° ffuller jun.	"
Jn°than ffuller	"
Joshua ffuller	"
Joseph ffuller	"
James Hawkes	Hingh.
Jos. Jacob	"
Enos. Kinsly	N. Hamp.
Peter Bracket	Biller.
C. R., Vol. V. p. 285.	

11 May 1681.

Tho. Eaton	Ded.
Natha. Chickering	"
Robe't Weare	"
David Hubbart	Hing.
Jerr. Beale	"
Tho. Hovey	Hadl.
Sam. Lancton	N. Hamp
Nath. Phelph	"
Benja. Gerrish	Salem
Ezekiol Cheevers	"
John Leech	"
Ephrajm Colton	Spr.
Tho. Colton	"
Joseph Stebbing	"
Joseph Trumble	"
Georg Norton	"

Sam. Kent	Glou.
Jn° Burbank	[?]
Wm. Starlinge	"
Sam. Peirson	"
Nath. Jewett	Conc.
Allen Bread sen'.	Lyn
Joseph Reads	"
Josiah Reads	"
Ephrajm Winship	Camb.
Abraham Tilton	Ips.
Isa. Esty	Tops.
Tho. Norman	"
C. R., Vol. V. p. 306.	

12 Oct. 1681.

Mr. Jn° Olliver 2 Ch. Bost.	
Tho. Chard	"
James Barnes	"
Hen. Bartholmew 1 Ch. B.	
Obadiah Sajle	"
Jn° Russells	Camb.
Jn° sen'.	"
Tho. Con	Ips.
Sam. Ingolls	"
Wm. Goodhue jun.	"
Jn° Pierson jun.	Row.
Jn° Sanyde (320)	"
John Whitman	Wey
Nicholas Whilmarsh	"
Steven ffrench	"
Jn° Bayly	"
Tho. Bayly	"
Rich'. Gurney	"
James Smith	"
Nathan Smith	"
Samuel Holbrooke	"
Wm. Richards jun.	"
Joseph Richards	"
Jn° Richards	"
Tho. Kingman	"
Samuel King	"
Wm. Read	"
Abijah Whitman	"
Tho. White	"
Joseph Dyer	"
Jn° Shaw jun.	"
Joseph Pitty	"
Tho. Noble	Wenh.
Eliaz' Weller	"
Sam. Ball	Spr.
Tho. Spencer	Suff'.
Tho. Stuksley (321)	"
C. R., Vol. V. pp. 320, 321.	

24 May 1682.

Jn° ffoster	Salem
Antho. Buxton	"
Peter Prescot	"
Mr. Jno. Apleton	Ips

Jn° Dane	Ips.
Jn° Wardner	"
Dani. Warner	"
Tho. Boreman	"
Joseph ffellows	"
Tho. Tredwell	"
Nath. Tredwell	"
Jos. far	Lyn
Jn° ffarrington	"
Humph. Barrat	Conc.
Sam. Haur	"
Roger Chandler	"
Sam. Stone	"
Sam. Kemball	Wenh.
Jn° Gilbert	"
Charl Got	"
Jn° Harding	Meadfei.
Jn° Warfeild	"
Benj. Clark	"
Jn° fisher	"
Sam Rockwood	"
Nath. Allin	"
Jn° Bates	Chelms.
Abra. Byam	"
Nath. Butterfeild	"
Abr. Parker	"
Isack Morrell	Chs.
Jn°than Caree	"
Sam. Bartlet	N. Hamp.
Jn° Pinor	Northfeild
C. R., Vol. V. p. 348.	

11 Oct. 1682.

Mr. Sam. Gardiner jun.	Salem.
Mr. Jn° Apleton	Ips.
Jn° Dane	"
Daniel Warner	"
Tho. Boreman	"
Joseph ffellows	"
Tho. Tredwell	"
Nath. Tredwell	"
Mr. Tho. Wade	"
Joseph Giddings	"
Joseph Safford	"
Wm Butler	"
Jn° Harding	Meadf.
Jn° Warfeild	"
Benja. Clarke	"
Jn° ffisher	"
Samuel Rockwood	"
Joseph Allin	"
Jn° fflegg	Watert"
Abra. Guile	"
Nath. Marcham	"
Wm. Band	"
Sam. Jeningson	"
Jn° farwell	Conc.
Tho. Browne jun.	"

LIST OF FREEMEN.

11 Oct. 1682.
Xtopher Walley   Conc.
James Parsons   Gloc.
Jnᵒ Hitchcock   Spr.
Josiah Gage   —
Joseph Kingsbery
Sam. Hasseltine
Sam. Stickney
Jnᵒ Bojnton
Wm. Hutchins
Benj. Kimball
Robert Hasseltine
Bozoun Allen
    C. R., Vol. V. p. 381

7 Feb. 1682–3.
Mr. Sam. Parris 1 Ch. Bost.
Mr. Adam Winthrop "
Mr. Robᵗ Howard   "
James Bill   "
John Olliver   "
Samuel Ruck   "
Obadia Wakfeild   "
Theoph. Rodes   "
Ebenezᵗ Wms   Dorch.
Nehemi. Clap   "
Jnᵒ Triscot   "
Jnᵒ Marshall   Biller.
David Meads   "
Dani. Lunt   Newb.
Daniel Merril   "
Wm. Moody   "
Jnᵒ Vyol   2 Ch. Bost.
Tho. Townsend   "
Samuel Townsend   "
James Green   "
John Green   "
Rich. Jincks   "
Timo. Pratt   "
Jnᵒ Andrews   Ips.
Josep. Browne   "
Sam. Pitcher   Milton.
    C. R., Vol. V. p. 383.

16 May 1683.
Jnᵒ Ingram   Hadley.
Mark Warner   "
Nathan. Warner   "
Jnᵒ Gardiner   "
Jnᵒthan Metcalfe   Dedh.
James feild   "
Georg March   Newb.
Humphry Horrel   Bevᵗʸ.
Edwᵈ Ashber   "
Jnᵒ Rayment   "
Wm. Raiment jun.   "

Andrew Elljot jun.   Bevᵗʸ.
Jnᵒ Dodge jun.   "
Wm. Dodg jun.   "
Tho. Woodbury   "
Edwᵈ Dodge   "
Henry Herricke   "
Mr. Jnᵒ Cobbitt   Ips.
Jose. Ewelle   "
Nath. Knolton   "
Mr. Grindall Rawson
                  Medfei.
Josiah Torrey   "
Dani. ffairfeild 1 Ch. Bost.
Samuell Ayres   Havˡˡ.
Jnᵒ Pickard jun.   Rowl.
Humph. Hobson   "
Sam. Allyn   N. Hamp.
Ebeneᵗ Strong   "
Sam. Wright   "
John Taylor   "
Jnᵒ Devereux   Marblehᵈ.
Tho. Pitman senᵗ.   "
Jnᵒ Peach jun.   "
Joseph Dallabar senᵗ. "
Wating James   "
Nicholas Andrew   "
Robert Bartlet   "
    C. R., Vol. V. p. 401.

13 Feb. 1683–4.
Mr. Edward Willis   Bost.
Tho. Ray   "
Henry Eames   "
Joseph Souther   "
Joseph Knight   New.
Tymothy Noys   "
James Jackman   "
Wm. Elsly   "
Josiah ffisher   Dedh.
Jnᵒthan ffreeman   "
Jonathan MedCalfe   "
James Vales   "
Joseph ffairbanks   "
John Colbrun   "
Peter Hansitt   "
Ralfe Dixe   Red.
    C. R., Vol. V. p. 427.

7 May 1684.
Chrispus Bruer   Lynn.
Henry Collins   "
Allen Bread   "
Joseph Roads   "
Jnᵒ Newhall   "
John Luise   "
Wm. Smith   "
Jonᵗʰ Selsbe   "

John Roads   Lynn.
Sam. Senden   Marblehead
Jnᵒ Merrit   "
Jose. Roote   N. Hamp.
Jonˢ Parsons   "
Wm. Holton   "
Robᵗ Lymon   "
Jnᵒ Hubbard   "
Jnᵒ Shelden   "
Benony Stebbins   "
Samˡˡ Judd   "
Jacob Root   "
Hen. Burt   "
Alexᵈʳ Atwood   "
Symon Burr   Hing.
francs James   "
Jnᵒ Mansfeild   "
Ephᵐ Nicholls   "
Increas Sykes   Sprᵈ.
Dani. Cooly   "
Danel Merrill   Newb.
Jnᵒ Bartlet   "
Josia Browne   Red.
Corneli. Browne   "
Tho. Nichols   "
Jnᵒ Hall   Rox.
Jnᵒ Whitney   "
Jnᵒ Dresser   Row.
Samˡˡ Palmer   "
Samˡˡ Peirce   Woob.
Samˡˡ Waters   "
Georg Read   "
Edwᵈ Johnson   "
Ebenezᵗ Johnson   "
    C. R., Vol. V. p. 436.

9 July 1684.
John Boynton   No. Hamp.
Tho. Hunt   "
John Dressar   Rowl.
James Dickinson   "
Richᵈ. Swan   "
Sam. Broclebank   "
James Seajles   "
Joseph Chaplin   "
Sam. Palmer   "
Samuel Platt   "
Sam. Spoffard   "
Jnᵒ Clarke   "
Joseph Jewet   "
Caleb Boynton   "
Nath. Jacob   "
Edwᵈ Walker   Woob.
Jnᵒ Holden   "
Joseph Peirce   "
Sam. Nogget   "

33

Phineas Upham	Woob.	Benja. Darse	Rox.
Jn° Savil	"	Peter Scott	Brant.
Sam. Savil	"	Sam. Basse	"
Theoph. Curtis	"	Nath. Wade	Mauld.
C. R., Vol. V. p. 447.		Ralfe Dixie	"
		Dani. Eaton	Redd.
10 Sept. 1684.		Jn°. Avesson	"
Sam. Porter	Hadley	ffran⁵ Hutchinson	"
Israel Porter jun.	"	Josh. Eaton	"
Jn° Hall	"	Jn° Abby sen'.	"
C. R., Vol. V. p. 453		Jn° ffiske	Wenh.
		Zackeus Goldsmith	"
31 Oct. 1684.		C. R., Vol. V. p. 476.	
Mr. James Lewis	1 Ch. B.		
David ffiske	Camb.	21 July 1685.	
Henry Prentice	"	Mr. Jn° Apleton jun.	Ips.
Ephrai. fïrost	"	Mr. Rob't Pajne jun.	"
Math. Peirse	Woob.	Abra. Purkins	"
Sam. Wilson	"	Jn° Harris (498)	"
Joseph Broune	Ips.	Jn° Graves	"
Wm. Hascall	——	Nath. Browne	"
Joseph Hascall		Jn° Maynard sen'.	Marlb.
Isaacke Eveleigh		Jn°th° Johnson sen'.	"
C. R., Vol. V. p. 458.		Josep: Newton	"
		Jn° Bowker	"
7 May 1685.		Tho. Braman	"
Urjah Clarke	Rox.	Jose. Millar	"
Thomas Mory	"	Noah Wiswall	Camb. Vill.

Edw⁴ Jackson	Camb. Vill.
Wm. Robinson	"
Joseph Wilson	"
Jn° Mirock	"
Sam. Truesdale	"
Isack Willjams	"
Jn° Ward	"
Wm. Pebody	Topsf.
Tho Perkins jun.	"
Dani. Reddington	"
Tobyah Perkins	"
Jocob ffoster	"
Jn° How	"
Edw⁴ Converse	Woob.
Ephraj. Pason	Dover
Tho. Sticknee	Bradf⁴.
Rich. Kemball (499)	
C. R., Vol. V. p. 498, 499.	
16 Feb. 1685–6.	
Jacob Toun'	Tops.
Ephraim Curtis	"
John Pritchet	"
Mr. Sam. Checkley	2 Ch.
John Squire	1 Ch.
Jacob Nash	Weym.
Jn° Burril	Lyn
C. R., Vol. V. p. 514.	

[During the usurpation by Andros, 1686–1689, the practice of admitting Freemen was discontinued: it was resumed after the Revolution, but with some modifications.]

12 Feb. 1689–90. "It is ordered by this Court, that the clause in the Law, title ffreemen, referring to Ministers giving certificate to persons desiring their ffreedom, be and hereby is repealed; and the sum of ten shillings is reduced to four shillings in a single Country Rate, (without heads of persons,) or that the person to be made free have houses or lands of the clear yearly value of six pounds, freehold, which value is to be returned to the Court by the Selectmen of the place or the major part of them, who also are to certify that such person is not vicious in life. And the additional Law, title ffreemen, made Oct. 15, 1673, is hereby likewise repealed."

C. R., Vol. VI. p. 114.

22 March 1689–90. "Sir William Phipps, Knt., Maj. General Wait Winthrop, Lt. William Bond, Daniel Andrews, Peter King, and Eben' Prout, admitted to be ffreemen, were sworn." *C. R., Vol. VI. p. 130.*

22 Mar. 1689–90. "Whereas divers returns are presented unto this Court of persons to be made free, the time being short before the nomination, Ordered, that all such persons allowed the privilege of freedom by this Court, may have the ffreeman's Oath administered unto them by any one Magistrate, and return thereof to be made to the Secretary."

C. R., Vol. VI. p. 130.

22 Mar. 1689–90. "Lists of the names of sundry persons from several Towns, qualified to be ffreemen, were presented and allowed of."

C. R., Vol. VI. p. 131.

[The Lists above-mentioned, and others which were subsequently presented, are contained in the volumes of the Massachusetts Archives, entitled Intercharter.]

22 March 1689-90.	Jacob Parker Malden	Joseph Collins sen' Lynn
Nathanael Wade Medford.	Simon Grover "	Jonaathan Selsbee "
Stephen Francis "	William Bucknam "	Crispus Brewer "
Jonathan Tuffts "	Thomas Burthen "	Jn°. Lynzey "
John Tuffts "	Joses Bucknam "	Saml. Edmonds "
John Whittimore "	Left. Samuell Sprague "	Allen Brade sen'. "
Intercharter, Vol. I. p. 295.	William Lerebe "	Josiah Rhoads "
(Cert.*) 11 March 1689-90.	Thomas Oaks "	Joseph Burrill "
Jn° Perrum Chelmsford.	Lazurus Grover "	Joseph Rhoades "
Joseph Perkis "	Joseph Lamson "	Joseph Newhall "
Nathll Butterfield "	Inter., Vol. I. p. 349.	Joseph ffarr "
Edward Spaulden "	15 May 1690.	John Ballard "
Joshuah ffletcher "	Jon* ffairbank Dedham.	Cornelius Browne "
Samll. ffletcher "	Jams Thorp "	Thomas ffarrar "
Will. ffletcher "	John Pidg "	Inter., Vol. I. p. 351.
John Spaulden "	John Everit "	22 March 1689-90.
Ely ffoster "	Samll. Everitt "	Abiah Sherman
Samll Cleavland "	John Hunting "	Watertown
Abrah. Parker "	Timot. Whiting "	Caleb Church "
Abraham Byam "	Danll Aullice "	Samll Edey "
Samll ffoster "	Asahail Smith "	Nick* Withe "
John Bates "	Eleazer Kingsbury "	Tho. Rider "
Inter., Vol. I. p. 349.	Michael Metcalf "	Samuell Marshall
22 March 1689-90.	Thom. ffuller "	Charlestown
Thomas Skinner jun.	Danll Pond "	Samll. Homan "
Malden	John Gay "	Eleaz'. Phillips "
Phinias Upam "	Nath. Bullard "	Inter., Vol. I. p. 351.
Nathaniell Upam "	John Alldis "	21 March 1689-90.
Phillip Atwood "	Danll ffisher "	Jams Minerd Concord
William Bordman "	Nath. Richards "	Danell Dane "
John Green "	Danll Wight "	Thomas Gobile "
Samuell Sprague jun. "	Amos ffisher "	Robord Blood "
Thomas Green "	Ralph Day "	John Wheler "
Nathaniell Dunnam "	Robert Awry "	Nemiah Hunt "
Obadia Jenkins "	Jon* Gay "	Samuell Davis "
John Chamberlen "	John ffuller "	John Shaperd "
Joseph Sargent "	Inter., Vol. I. p. 350.	Abraham Tempel "
William Tell "	16 May 1690.	Recherd Tempel "
Thomas Grover "	William Stevens	Isaac Tempel "
John Sargent sen'. "	Gloucester.	Simon Davis "
Joseph Wayte "	Timothy Day "	Robard Blood "
Edward Marshell "	Jephrey Passens "	Simon Blood "
Samuell Green "	John Passens "	Josiah Blood "
John Sprague jun. "	Edward Huse "	Judath Poter "
Thomas Newall "	Thomas Kent "	John Jones "
Left.—Willson "	Joseph Mason Watertown	Nathanell Stow "
Isak Hill "	John Warren jun. "	Nathaell Harwood "
Jonathan Sprague "	Thomas Straite "	Eliphelet fox "
James Chadwick "	Samuel Biggilo "	John Ball "
Joseph floyd "	Inter., Vol. I. p. 350.	Samuell flecher "
John floyd "	[No date.]	Timithy Ries "
Nathaniell Howard "	Lt. John Burrill sen'. Lynn	Samuell Stratten "
Phinias Sprague "	Jn° Burrill jun'. "	Johnethen Habord "
Sargent — fosdick "	Jn°. Hawcks sen'. "	Joshua Wheler "
Jacob Winslad "	Henry Collins sen'. "	James Smally "
Benjamin Whitamore "	Wm. Smith "	Nathanell Brise "
Jonathan Knohre "	Moses Haven "	John Wood "

* Certified by Selectmen, as entitled to Freedom.

Abraham Wood Concord
Obadiah Wheler "
John Haward "
Thomas Wheler "
Steven Hosmer "
John Hartwill "
 Inter., Vol. I. p. 352.
 22 March 1689–90.
Lt. Simon Davis Concord
Lt. Jonathan Prescot "
Joseph ffrench "
Thomas Pellet "
Samuel Hunt "
Eliezer fflag "
Samuel Hartwell "
Samuel Myriam "
John Wheeler "
Samuel How "
Abraham Tayler "
John Hayward "
Nathaniel Ball "
Samuel Wheate "
Timothy Wheeler "
John Myriam "
Daniel Pellet "
John Pearly Boxford
Thomas Redington "
Joseph Byxbe "
Samuell Symonds "
Daniell Wood "
Abraham Redington "
John Kimball "
Thomas Andrew "
Joseph Andrew "
Thomas Hazzen "
Mr. William Perkins
 Topsfield
Mr. Timothy Perkins "
Corp'. Samuel Standley
 Topsfield
Sarg'. John Henry "
Corp'. John Curtiss "
Joseph Townes sen'. (353)
 Topsfield
Nathanael Ingersoll
 Salem Village
Abraham Walcott "
Zechariah Goodale sen'.
 Salem Village
Edward Putman "
Tho. Wilkins sen'. "
John Putman secundus
 Salem Village
Henry Wilkins "
Aaron Way "
Benj' Wilkins "
James Putman "
Sam : Sibly "
John Tarbell "
Benj'. Putman "

Jonathan Putman
 Salem Village
Samuel Nurse "
William Way "
Samuel Abbie "
Mr. Daniel Andrew "
Henry Bowen Roxbury
Joshua Sever "
Samuel Gore "
Samuel Payson "
Isaac How "
John Scott "
Mr. Neh. Walter "
Tho. Moore (360) "
 Inter., Vol. I. pp. 353, 360.
 18 April 1690.
Cap'. Jonathan Walcott
 Salem Village
Ensign Thomas fflint
 Salem Village
Serg'. Job Swinaton "
Serg'. John Buxton "
Mr. Joseph Hutchinson
 sen'. Salem Village
Joseph Holton sen'. "
Joseph Holton jun'. "
Joseph Pope "
John fflint "
William Sibley "
William Osburn "
Thomas Haines "
Thomas ffuller jun'. "
Jacob ffuller "
Edward Bishop sen'.
 Salem Village
Thomas Rayment "
Joshua Rea jun'. "
Walter Phillips sen'.
 Salem Village
ffrances Nurs sen'. "
Thomas Preston "
Joseph fflint "
Benjamine ffuller (12)
 Salem Village
Mr. Israell Porter "
Rob'. Gibbs "
Joseph Herrick "
Cap'.Nath".Norden "
Cap'. Jn°. Pitman "
Mr. Benj. Gale "
Wm. Woods (13) "
Peter Gardner Roxbury
Mr. John Howard "
Edmund Weld "
John Hemmingway "
John Newel "
Benjamin Gamblin "
Jacob Newel "
Josiah Holland "
Jams ffrissel "

John Griggs Rox.
Samuel Perry "
Jams Draper sen'. "
Thomas Cheiny "
John Holbrook "
Samuel Weld "
Isaac How "
John Ruggles 2ᵈ "
William Heath "
Jonathan Peake "
John May "
John Perram "
Isaac Morriss "
Jacob Chamberlain "
John Bugbey "
Mr. William Denison "
Benjamin Dowse "
John Davis "
John Lyon (14) "
 Inter., Vol. II. pp. 12–14.
 (Cert.) 26 March 1690.
John ffuller sen'.
 NewCambridge
Nathaniell Willson sen'.
 NewCambridge
James Prentis sen'. "
John Mason "
John Kennarick "
John Hide "
Seabis Jackson "
Abraham Jackson "
Nathaniel Hamond "
Thomas Greenwood "
Nathaniell Helie "
John Ward "
William Ward "
Jacob Bacon "
Ebenezer Stone "
William Hide "
Eliezer Hide "
Edward Jakson "
Steeven Cook "
 Inter., Vol. II. p. 20.
 18 April 1690.
Beniamin Weeb Malden
Tryall Newbery "
Samuell Wayt "
John Mudg "
Samuell Oldum Cambridge
Nathaniell Robbins "
Samuell Robbins (20)
 Cambridge
Josiah Jons Watertown
John Livermore "
Thomas Woolson "
Joseph Gearfield "
Josiah Treadway "
John Woodward "
Benjamin Willington "

John Bond Watertown	Nath. Page Billerica	Ephraim Brown Salisbury
John ffisske "	John Trull sen'. "	James Carre "
Joseph Herington "	Daniel Shead juni. "	Solomon Shepard "
Thomas Hammon "	Sam¹ frost "	Nath¹¹ Whitcher "
Mihell Barsto "	Jonath. Danforth juni. "	Abraham Brown "
Joseph Peirce sen'. "	John Wilson sen'. "	John Clough s'. "
John Begolo sen'. "	Cornet John Lane "	John Clough jr. "
John Wright "	James Pattison "	Richard Smith "
Daniel Herington "	John Baldwin "	Meros Tucker "
Rodger Willington "	Caleb farle sen'. "	Jereme Allin "
William Shattuck "	John Marshall "	Nath¹¹ Eastman "
John Genery "	Joseph foster "	Jacob Morrell "
John Parkhust "	Jonath. Hill "	Jarvis Ringe "
Nathaniel Bright "	Henry Jefts juni. "	John Allin "
Samuel Hager "	Jn°. Rogers "	Mr. Rob' Pike jr. "
Palsgrave Willington "	Joshua Sawyer Woburn	Joseph True "
Thomas Herington "	Nath¹¹ Richardson "	Benjamin Estman (25)
Nathaniel Bond "	Will. Wyman "	Salisbury
John Kimboll "	Jacob Wyman "	Charls Davenport
Jonathan Smith (21) "	Steven Richardson "	Dorchester
Mr. John Bisco "	Josiah Wood "	Samuel Pason "
Mr. Willyam Godard "	Benj. Simonds "	Henry Garnsy "
Samuell Thatcher "	Caleb Symonds "	John Blacke "
John Bacon "	Sam. Blogget "	John Breeck "
Thomas Whitny "	Georg Reed "	Ebenezer Billings "
Richard Chilld jun'. "	Henry Sumers "	Thomas Trott jun'. "
Beniamin Pearse "	John Peirce "	Peeter Lion "
Joseph Undurwoode "	Georg Brush "	Standfast foster "
Thomas Kidur "	Jonathan Wyman "	Daved Joans "
Richard Cuttin sen'. "	Seth Wyman (22) "	Daniel Preston "
Henary Spring jun'. "	Eleazer Bateman "	Noah Beman "
Jonathan Stimson "	Joseph Right jun'. (24)	Ephraim Pason "
Samuell Begaloo "	Woburn	Thomas Andrews "
Beniamin ffleg "	*Inter., Vol. II. pp. 22–24.*	James Backer "
Beniamin Garfilld "	18 April 1690.	Thomas Bird "
Richard Chilld "		James Bird "
Dannill Warrin (22) "	Mr. Will. Hooke Salisbury	Richerd Butt "
Inter., Vol. II. pp. 20–22.	Mr. Tho. Mudget "	John Blackman "
[No date.]	Will. Osgood "	Hopstill Humphry "
Mr Samuell Gookin	Danell Mondy "	Samuel Hall "
Cambridge	Philip Grele "	Richerd Evins "
Nicholas ffesenden "	Joseph Eaton "	Isack Humphry "
Peter Town "	Simon ffrench "	John Minot "
William Munroe "	Isaac Buswell "	Gorg Minot "
John Squire "	Ephraim Severano "	William Rossen "
John Oldam "	Sam¹¹ ffelows jun'. "	Samuel Robinson "
Jacob Hill "	Sam¹¹ Estman "	James Robinson "
Sam¹¹ Gibson "	Joseph fflecther "	Isack Riall "
John Wieth "	Benⁱʰ Allin "	Samuel Sumner "
William Wieth "	Sam¹¹ Gill "	Ebenezer Withington
Henry Smith "	Andrew Grele "	Dorchester
Tho. Andrew "	Isaac Grene "	Phillep Withington "
Samuell Sparhawke "	Philip fflanders "	Samuel Wals (26) "
Nathaniell Sparhawk	Will. Allin "	Obediah Ward
Cambridge	Richard Hubard "	Marlborough
Inter., Vol. II. p. 22.	L : John Stevens "	Thomas How "
18 April 1690.	E : Nath¹¹ Brown "	Increas Ward "
Capt. Ralph Hill Billerica	Joshua Bayle "	John Newtten "
John Starns "	John fflanders "	John Mainerd sen'. "
	Sam¹¹ ffowlerer "	Isace How "

Thomas Brigham   Marlb.
John fay   "
James Woods   "
John Brigham   "
John Barnes   "
John Jonson   "
Samuell Brigham   "
Richard Barns   "
Thomas Rice   "
Johnathan Jonson   "
Isace Amsden   "
John Barritte   "
Samuell Goodenew   "
Nathanell Josline   "
Nathanell Jonson   "
Eliazer How   "
Thomas Martine   "
Joshua Rice   "
Moses Newtten(27)   "
Inter., Vol. II. pp. 25–27.

22 March 1689–90.

S^r. William Phipps
    [not stated.]
Major Genl. Winthrop
    [not stated.]
Mr. Charles Morton "
Lt. William Bond   "
Dan. Andrew   "
Abraham Jones   "
Samuel Symonds   "
Phinehas Sprague   "
Ebenezar Prout   "
John Foster   "
Peter Sergeant   "
Mr. John Aires   "
Mr. Nathaniel Oliver
    [not stated.]
Mr. Pyam Blower   "
Tim. Philips   "
Peter King   "
Mr. Edwd. Brumfeild "
Mr. Simeon Stoddard "
Mr. Joseph Parsons "
Capt. Thomas Savage "
Mr. Sam^u. Linde (60) "
John Comes   "
Thomas Savage, goldsmith
    [not stated.]
John Clow   "
Ezek. Clesby   "
Joseph Belknap   "
Capt. Sam^u. Legg   "
Capt. Wm. Clarke   "
Capt. Peter Buteler "
Mr. Joseph Prout   "
Mr. Samson Stoddard
    [not stated.]
Mr. Wm. Clutterbucke
    [not stated.]
Mr. Robt. Bronsdon "

Mr. Rich^d. Middlecott
    [not stated.]
Mr. Benj^a. Alford   "
Mr. Benj^a. Davis(61) "
    Inter., Vol. II. pp. 60, 61.

15 May 1690.

Mr. John Eyers   Boston
Jeremiah Bumsted   "
Roger Judd   "
Mr. James Olliver   "
Mr. William Brattle   "
Joseph Squire   "
Mr. Benja. Davis   "
Mr. Nath^u. Olliver   "
Mr. Sam^{ll} Chicklie   "
John Nicholes   "
Richard Draper   "
John Eastmond   "
Robert Hussey   "
Will. Downinge   "
Mr. Joseph Bosset   "
Joseph Holmes   "
James Dunny   "
Joseph Belknap   "
Mr. Daniell Quinsey   "
George Elistone   "
Robt. Hawkins   "
Sam^{ll} Oake   "
Josiah Grise   "
Sam^{ll} Grise   "
John Marshall   "
Mr. Peter Sergeant   "
Ebenez^r Hayden   "
Eleazer Moody   "
Daniell Olliver   "
John Conniball   "
William Manley   "
John Proctor   "
Jeremiah Belchar   "
James Halsey   "
John Carthew   "
Thomas Walker   "
Tymothy Wadsworth   "
Major Tho. Savage   "
Thomas Cushan   "
Richard Procter   "
Capt. William White   "
Mr. Rich^d. Middlecott   "
Mr. Benj^a Alford   "
James Greene   "
Thomas Atkins   "
Nathan^{ll}. Thayer   "
Sam^{ll}. Townsend (61) "
Thomas Harwood   "
Joseph Briscoe   "
Sam^{ll} Townsend jun.   "
Joseph Ustice   "
Jeremiah ffitch   "
Roger Kilcup   "
Samuell Rucke sen^r.   "

John Greene   Boston
Henery Dawson   "
Hezechiah Hinksman   "
Nathaniell Hinksman   "
Michaell Shaller   "
George Hallet sen^r.   "
John Addams   "
Isaac Goose   "
Mr. Thomas Brattle   "
Richard Wilkins   "
Benjamen Pemberton   "
Phillip Squire   "
Ellis Calender   "
Thomas Skiner   "
Grimstone Bond   "
Samuell Jackline   "
William Clough   "
Jarvis Ballard   "
John Wiswall   "
Joseph Bill   "
John Tuttle   "
Edward Tuttle   "
Elisha Tuttle   "
Jonathan Tuttle   "
Isack Lewis   "
Elias Mavericke   "
Joseph Hasey   "
Thomas Jackson (62) "
    Inter., Vol. II. pp. 61, 62.

30 May 1690.

Capt. Jno. Allice   Hatfield
Ens. Dan^{ll} White   "
Sam^{ll} Marsh   "
John Wells   "
John ffeild   "
Stephen Genings   "
John Cowels   "
Nath^{ll} Dickenson sen^r. "
Richd Morton sen^r.   "
Sam^{ll} Dickenson sen^r. "
John White   "
John Porter   Hadley
John John Smith   "
Saml Philip Smith   "
Joseph Smith   "
Saml. Chiliab Smith   "
Hezekiah Porter   "
Danl. Hubbard   "
John Philip Smith   "
Nehemiah Dickenson   "
Jonathan Marsh   "
Peter Montague   "
Daniall Marsh   "
Nathill White   "
John Goodman   "
Jacob Warner   "
    Inter., Vol. II. p. 91.

30 May 1690.

Serg^t Joseph Coker Newb.

Joseph Bayley — Newbury
Isack Bayley — "
Cornet Jonathan Moores — Newbury
John Worth — "
Steaphen Jcques — "
Silvanus Plum' — "
John Emery jun'. — "
Serg.' Jn°. Hall — "
Jn°. Webster jun'. — "
Richard Dodg — Wenham
James ffreind — "
Tho'. ffiske jun'. — "
John Dodg jun'. — "
Wm. ffairefield — "
Ephraim Kemball — "
Zecheas Gooldsmith — "
John Edwards — "
Walter ffairfield — "
John Porter (103) — "
John Person — Northampton
Thomas Limon — "
Hezekiah Root — "
Abell Jones — "
Richerd Limon — "
William Miller sen'. — "
Israell Rust — "
Sam". Holton — "
Sam". Marshal — "
Noah Cook — "
Joseph Edwords — "
Sam" Edwords — "
Jedediah Strong — "
Ensigne Pr' Clap — "
John Seorls — "
Isack Shelden jun'. — "
Jonathan Root — "
John Limon, weav'. — "
John Limon, shoemaker — Northampton
Ebnezer Allord — "
Ebenezer Wright — "
Nathaniel Edwards — "
Mathew Clefton — "
William Clarke jr. — "
William Phelps — "
Samuel Smith — "
Samuel Parsons — "
John Alexander — "
William Southwell — "
Samuel Curtis — "
Philip Pain — "
Samuel Wright — "
Thomas Sheilden — "
Mr. Wareham Mather — Northampton
Nathaniel Alexander — Northampton
John King jun'. — "
Joseph Wright — "

Joseph Crosbey — Braintree
John Adams — "
Samuel Payn — "
Robert feild — "
John Bass jun'. — "
Wiliam Nightingall jun'. — "
  (104) Braintree
Inter., Vol. II. pp. 103,104.

— October 1690.

Mosis Tiler — Boxford
Nathaniel Browen — "
Daniel Wood — "
John Stiels — "
John Pearly — "
Joseph Pebody — "
John Andrus — "
Inter., Vol. II. p. 179.

19 December 1690.

Thomas Cooper — Springfield
Abel Wright sen'. — "
Nathan". Burt sen'. — "
Jn°. Blisse — "
John Dorchester — "
James Dorchester — "
Eliakim Cooley — "
Benja. Cooley — "
Joseph Cooley — "
Joseph Leonard — "
Joseph Bedortha — "
Edward ffoster — "
Samuel Stebbins — "
Joseph Thomas — "
Thomas Day jun'. — "
John Mirricke — "
Sam" Bliss jun'. — "
Nathan". Blisse — "
Jonatha. Morgan — "
David Morgan — "
James Barker — "
Sam" Bedortha — "
Benja. Leonard — "
Jonathan Ball — "
John Harman — "
Joseph Ely — "
John Burt — "
Samuell Lamb — "
Josias Marshfield — "
Thomas Stebbins — "
Edward Stebbins — "
Benjamin Stebbins — "
Jonathan Burt jun'. — "
David Lumbard — "
Isaac Colton — "
John Colton — "
Sam" Blisse 3ᵗⁱᵘˢ — "
Samuel Miller — "
John Miller — "
Tho. Swetnam — "

Charles fferrey — Springfield
Daniel Lamb — "
Inter., Vol. II. p. 255.

24 December 1690.

Capt. Tho. Harvy — Amesbury
John Barnard — "
John foot — "
Thomas Sarjant — "
Thomas Barnard sen'. — "
Thomas Curriar — "
Nathan Gould — "
Thomas Colby sen'. — "
Thomas Steevens — "
Thomas fowlar — "
Joseph Lankestar sen'. — Amesbury
Henry Blazdell sen'. — "
Henry Tuksbery sen'. — Amesbury
Jn°. Kimball — "
Moses Morrel — "
Orlando Bagley — "
Inter., Vol. II. p. 257.

6 February 1690–1.

John Emerson jun'. — Gloucester
C. R., Vol. VI. p. 174.

18 April 1691.

John Maston sen'. — Andover
William Blunt — "
John Abbute — "
William Lovioy — "
Hopstill Tyler — "
John Tyler — "
Steven Porter — "
Gorge Abbute — "
Joseph Lovioy — "
Samuel Hoult — "
Robberd Russell — "
Thomas Johnson — "
ffranses Deane — "
John Bridges — "
James ffrie — "
William Johnson — "
Walltar Witt — "
Andruw ffoster — "
Joseph Robinson — "
Edward Phelps — "
John Osgood jun'. — "
John Russe — "
Timothy Osgood — "
Mr. Jonathan Woodman — [Newbu. ?]
Thomas Hull — "
Jonathan Emery — "
Inter., Vol. III. p. 9.

(Cert.) 6 April 1691.
Samuell Johnson sen'.
            Boston
John Bull sen'.   "
Jabes Neges   "
Sam" Marshall   "
James English   "
David Jenner   "
    Inter., Vol. III. p. 9.
18 April 1691.
John Whitmarsh
         Weymouth
Joseph Drake   "
Incres Bates   "
Thomas Randol   "
John Randol   "
John Blanchar   "
Joseph Shawe   "
Epharem Borell .   "
    Inter., Vol. III. p. 10.
(Cert.) 26 March 1691.
Ens. John Woods
         Marlborough
Samuel Ward   "
Joseph Newton sen'.
         Marlborough
John Bouker   "
    Inter., Vol. III. p. 10.
18 April 1691.
Joshuah Eaton   Reading
Jonathan Eaton   "
Thomas Damman   "
John Nickols   "
James Nickols   "
Nathanell Parker   "
Samuell Damman   "
John Burnap   "
John Boutwell   "
Richard Harden   "
Jonas Eaton   "
Josepth Hartshorne   "
John Woodward   "
Thomas Nickols   "
Beniamin Hartshorne
         Reading
Nathanell Gouen   "
Samuell Smith   "

David Hartshorne Reading
John Parker   "
Timothy Hartshorne "
Jerimiah Swaine   "
John Browne   "
Cornelius Browne   "
William Eaton   "
Thomas Burnap   "
John Wesson   "
William Arnall   "
ffrances Huchison   "
Timothy Wilely   "
Josepth Burnap   "
John Eaton   "
William Robbins   "
Samuel Lilly   "
Robbart Burnap   "
John Uptan sen'.   "
Gorge fflint   "
David Bacheller   "
John Dunton   "
John Dix   "
ffrances Smith (10)   "
Lieu".   Lewis   Lynn
Mr.   Habersfeild   "
Thomas ffarrar jun'.   "
Joseph Meriam   "
Will". Merriam   "
Ebenezer Hathorn   "
John Edmunds   "
Rich'. Hood sen'.   "
John Ingols sen'.   "
Rob'. Ingolls   "
Benjam". ffar   "
Henry Collins jun'.   "
Daniell Hithins sen'.   "
John Burrill 2ᵈ   "
Ebenezer Stocker   "
Moses Hawks   "
Thomas Baker   "
Benjam" Rednap   "
Thomas Jovory   "
Joseph Mansfeild jun'.   "
Rob'. Potteʳ jun'.   "
Eleazer Lynzy   "
Will" ffarrington   "
John Newhall sen'.   "
Aquilla Ramsdell   "
Theophilus Bayley   "

Cornet   Johnson   Lynn
Daniell Mansfeild   "
Thomas Graves, sen'.   "
Samu". Graves   "
Rob'. Rand jun'.   "
Samuell Moors   "
Nathaniell Ballard   "
John Bread   "
Daniell Needham   "
Thomas Chadwell   "
Joseph Bread   "
Allin Bread 3ᵗⁱᵘˢ   "
Timothy Bread   "
Mathew ffarrington jun'.
         Lynn
Nathaniell Newhall senʳ
         Lynn
Sam". Hort   "
Joseph Hort   "
Richard Haven sen'.   "
Robert Paffer sen'.   "
Jonathan Hudson   "
Moses Hudson   "
John Moor   "
Edward ffuller   "
Samu" Rhodes   "
Ensign John Newhall   "
Andrew Townsend   "
Andrew Mansfeild   "
Will". Bassett sen'.   "
Willa". Bassett jun'.   "
John Lewis jun'.   "
Sam". Jynks   "
Nathan Newhall jun'.   "
Benjam". Collins   "
John Richards   "
John Diven   "
Ens. Edwᵈ. Baker   "
Thomas Lewis   "
Samuell Ingolls   "
Henry Collins jun'.   "
John Jynks (11)   "
Joseph Mansfeild jun'.   "
Josiah Rhodes   "
Richard Hood   "
Theophilus ffarrington   "
Samuel Bligh (12)   "
    Inter., Vol. III. pp. 10–12.

Wm. 30
Avesson, Jno. 34
Awry, Robert 35
Ayer, Peter 25
  Robrt. 28
  Tho. 25
Ayres, Samuell 33

--- B ---

Babb, Phillip 23
Babridge, Xtopher 25
Bacheller, David 40
Bachiler, Joseph 15
  Willi. 20
Bachilor, John 17
Backer, James 37
Bacon, Francis 25
  Jacob 36
  James 29
  John 37
Badger, John 29
Bagley, Orlando 39
Bailey, Jno. 28
Baker, Alex. 21
  Edward 16
  Edwd., Ens. 40
  Jno. 31
  John 12, 18 (2), 19, 23, 28
  Nicholas 14
  Richrd. 19
  Sam. 31
  Tho. 25
  Thom. 22
  Thomas 40
  Timo. 30
  Willm 13
Bakor, John 21
Balch, Jno. 31
Balche, John 11
Baldin, Jno. 27
Balduin, Joseph 25
  John 37
  Joseph 27 (2)
Baldwine, Hen. 22
Bale, Nathaniell 22
Ball, Eliar. 31
  John 22, 35
  Jonathan 39
  Nathaniel 36
  Richard 23
  Sam. 32
Ballard, Jarvis 38
  John 35
  Nathaniell 40
  Sam. 32
  William 16
Balshe, John 10
Balstone, Will. 10
  Willm 11
Bambridge, Guy 13
Banckes, Rich. 23
Bancroft, Roger 19
Band, Wm. 32
Bankroft, Tho. 31
Bapson, James 25
Barber, Geo. 21
  Jno. 27
Barbore, Richrd. 18
Barcker, James 18
Barker, James 39
  John 28, 29
  Nath. 30
  Thoma. 17
  Wm. 30

Barkr., Tho. 30
Barlow, George 23
Barnard, Jno. 27, 30
  John 39
  Math. 28
  Thomas, senr. 39
Barnes, James 32
  John 38
  Nathani 30
  Tho. 28
  Thom. 21
  William 18
Barny, Jacob 12
Barrat, Humph. 32
  Humphry 24
Barrell, Geo. 20
Barret, John, senr. 23
  Joseph 30
Barrett, Jno., juni. 23
Barrill, Thom. 20
Barritte, John 38
Barrone, Eliis 18
Barsham, Will. 15
Barsto, Mihell 37
Bartelmew, Richrd. 18
Bartholmew, Hen. 32
Bartholmewe, Will. 13
Bartholomewe, Henry 15
Bartlet, Jno. 33
  Jno., jun. 26
  John 15
  Rich., jun. 30
  Robert 33
  Sam. 28, 32
Bartlett, Thomas 13
Bartol, Wm. 27
Barton, Edward 29
Bascome, Tho. 27
Bass, John, junr. 39
Basse, Sam. 34
  Samll. 12
  Samu. 21
  Tho. 24
Bassett, Willam., junr. 40
  Willm., senr. 40
Bastowe, Michaell 14
Batchelor, Jno. 25
  Nath. 26
Batchelr., John 13
  Steven 14
Batchiler, Jno. 27
  Marke 24
Bate, Benj. 28
  Clement 28
  George 14
  James 14, 28
  Joseph 28
  Samuell 28
Bateman, Eleazer 37
  Thomas 19
  Willi. 18
  Willm 11
Bates, Clemt. 14
  Edward 15, 16
  Incres 40
  Jno. 32
  John 35
Batsons, Steven 23
Batt, Nicho. 27
  Paul 28
  Timothy 28
Batte, Christopher 16
Batter, Edmond 14
  Nicholas 16
Battle, Tho. 23
Baxter, Gregory 11
Bayle, Joshua 37

Bayley, Isack 39
  Jno. 26
  John 26
  Joseph 39
  Theophilus 40
Bayly, Henry 27
  James 28
  Jno. 26, 30, 32
  Jonas 24
  Mary 22
  Tho. 26, 32 (2)
  Thom. 17
Beachamp, Edwa. 20
Beadseley, Will. 14
Beale, Caleb 28
  Jacob 28
  Jerr. 32
  Jno. 28
  John 16
  Thom. 15
Beales, Jer. 24
Beard, Aaron 29
  Tho. 27
  Thom. 20
Beares, Richrd. 15
Becke, Alex. 13
Bedortha, Joseph 39
  Samll. 39
Beecher, Tho. 11
Beers, Anthony 24
Begaloo, Samuell 37
Begolo, John, senr. 37
Belchar, Edw. 11
  Gregory 18
  Jeremiah 38
Belcher, Jeremy 16
  Moses 27
Belden, Sam. 28
Belknap, Joseph 25,38 (2)
Bell, Thom. 14
Bellingham, Richrd. 14
  Willi. 18
Beman, Noah 37
Bendall, Edw. 12
Benham, John 10, 11
Beniamin, John 11
Benjamin, Jno. 25, 26
Bennet, Edward 14
  James 16
  Rich. 28
Benseley, Will. 14
Benson, Joseph 31
Bent, John 17
Bernard, Franc. 25
  John 13 (2)
Berry, Willi. 19
Bessell, Jno. 29
Betsham, Richrd. 15
Bickford, George 29
  Jno., sen. 27
Bidfeild, Samu. 18
Biggilo, Samuel 35
Biggs, John 12
Bill, James 33
  Joseph 38
  Tho. 27
Billindg, Roger 20
Billing, Jno. 24
  Natha. 18
Billings, Ebenezer 37
  Nathan. 28
Bingley, Tho. 28
Bircher, Thom. 15
Bird, James 37
  John 21, 28
  Symon 20
  Thomas 37
Bisco, John 37

43

Bishop, Edward, senr. 36
 Natha. 20
 Bishope, Richrd. 19
Bishopp, Townsend 14
Black, John 27
Blackborne, Walter 17
Blacke, Henry 20
 John 11, 37
 Rich. 20
Blackeleach, John 13
Blackestone, Willm 10
Blackman, Jno. 25
 John 37
Blackstone, Will. 10
Blake, Edw. 25
 James 22, 30
 John 20
 William 16
 Wm. 22
Blanchar, John 40
Blanchard, John 22
 Willi. 18
Blanton, Willi. 20
Blany, Jno. 30
Blatt, Jno. 31
Blazdell, Henry 39
Bligh, Samuel 40
 Tho. 29
Blindman, Richard 19
Bliss, Samll., junr. 39
Blisse, Jno. 39
 Nathanll. 39
 Samll., 3tius. 39
 Thom. 19
Bloget, Dan. 22
Blogget, Sam. 37
Bloise, Edmond 17
Blood, James 19
 Josiah 35
 Roberd 35
 Robord 35
 Simon 35
Blott, Robte 13
Blower, Pyam 38
Bloyce, Franc. 19
Bloyett, Thomas 14
Blumfeild, Willm 14
Blunt, William 39
Boade, Henry 23
Boardman, Andrew 29, 30
Boden, Ambros, senr. 24
 Ambrose 24
Bointon, Willi. 17
Bojnton, Jno. 33
Bond, Grimstone 38
 John 37
 Nathaniel 37
 Niccolas 23
 William, Lt. 34, 38
Bonighton, Jno. 24
Bootefishe, Robte 14
Booth, Robert 23
 Symon 31
Bordman, William 35
 Wm. 22
Borell, Epharem 40
Boreman, Tho. 13, 32 (2)
Bosset, Joseph 38
Bosworth, Ben. 25
 Benj. 28, 31
 John 12
 Jose. 31
 Nathani. 31
 Zacheus 14
Bouker, John 40
Boules, Joseph 23
Boulter, Rich. 22, 24
Boulton, Nicho. 20

Bounde, Willi. 15
Bourne, Jarrett 13
 Nehemi. 18
Boutwell', James 16
 John 40
Bowelis, John 17
Bowen, Griffin 16
 Henry 36
Bowker, Jno. 34
Bowles, Jno. 31
Bowman, Nath. 10
Bowstreete, Willi. 16
Boyden, Thom. 21
Boynton, Caleb 33
 John 33
 Joseph 30
Boyse, Joseph 19
 Mathewe 17
Bracket, James 28, 30
 Jno. 25, 27
 Peter 20, 32
 Richrd. 14
Bradberry, Thom. 17
Bradbuth, Robt. 31
Brade, Allen, senr. 35
Bradeway, Richard 29
Bradford, Moses 26
 Robrt. 19
Bradshaw, Humphry 28
Bradstreet, Dudley 29
 Sam. 24
Bradstreete, Humfry 13
 Symon 14
Bragdon, Arthur 23
Brakenbury, Rich. 12
 Sam. 28
 Willm 12
Braman, Tho. 34
Brancen, George 23
Branch, Willi. 21
Brand, Andrew 24
 Ben. 10
 Goerge 22
Brandishe, John 13
Branker, John 11
Brarboun, Jno. 30
Brattle, Thomas 38
 William 38
Bread, Allen 33
 Allen, senr. 32
 Allin, 3tius. 40
 John 40
 Joseph 40
 Timothy 40
Breck, Edward 17
Breeck, John 37
Brenton, Willm 12
Breuster, Jno. 28
Brewar, Tho. 22
Brewer, Crispus 35
 Daniell 12
 Jno. 31
 Nathaniel 29
 Obedi. 19
Brick, Robrt. 21
Bridge, Edmond 17
 Edward 17
 John 13
 Sam. 28
 Samuel 28
Bridges, John 39
 Mathias 28
 Robrt. 18
 Wm. 21
Bridgham, Hen. 20
 Jnothn. 30
 Joseph 30
Bridgman, Jno. 30

Brigden, Tho. 14
Briggam, Thomas 15
Brigham, John 38
 Thomas 38
Bright, Henry 13
 Jno. 27
 Nathaniel 37
 Sam. 21
Brike, Mannasseth 27
Brinsmead, Wm. 27
Brinsmeade, John 15
Brisco, Willi. 18
Briscoe, Joseph 38
Brise, Nathanell 35
Briskow, Dani. 19
Broàd, Allin 27
Brock, John 19
Broclebank, Sam. 33
Bronsdon, Robt. 38
Brooke, Caleb 23
 Henry 16
 Joshua 22
 Thomas 14
Brookes, Isack 28
 John 22
Brooks, Gershom 28
Broune, Jabez 31
 Joseph 34
Browen, Nathaniel 39
Brown, Abraham 37
 Ephraim 37
 Nathll., E. 37
Browne, Abraham 11, 24
 Boaz 26, 29
 Corneli. 33
 Cornelius 35, 40
 Edmond 17, 22
 Edward 18
 Eliazer 29
 Eward 13
 Francis 28, 29
 George 17
 James 12,' 14, 15, 25
 Jno. 26
 John 13, 16, 31, 40
 Jonatha. 26
 Josep. 33
 Joseph 28
 Joshua 28
 Josia 33
 Nath. 34
 Nicholas 16
 Rich. 10 (2), 13
 Robrt. 21
 Tho. 25
 Tho., jun. 32
 Thom. 26
 Thomas 16 (2)
 Willi. 18, 21
 Wm., jr. 25
Browninge, Thom. 15
Bruer, Chrispus 33
Brumfeild, Edwd. 38
Brush, Georg 37
Bry, Phillip 29
Bryant, Abra. 28
Buck, James 17
Buckford, Wm. 29
Buckland, Tho. 14
Buckmr., Tho. 21
Bucknam, Joses 35
 William 35
Bucknell, Georg 29
 Richard 29
Bugbey, John 36
Bugby, Rich. 10, 11
Bulckley, Edmond 13
Bulfinch, John 19

Coalborne, Nathani. 18
Cobbet, Samuel 29
  Thomas 16
Cobbitt, Jno. 33
  Josias 18
Cock, Jno. 29
Cockeram, Willi. 16
Coddington, Will. 14
Codogan, Ricd. 23
Coe, Robte 13
Coffin, Tristram 26
Coffyn, James 27
  Peter 26
Cogeswell, John 14
Coggan, John, juni. 19
Coggeshall, Jo. 11
Coggin, John 12
Coker, Joseph, Sergt. 38
Colbran, Wm. 10
Colbron, Will. 10
Colbrun, John 33
Colby, Anthony 12
  Thomas, senr. 39
Coldam, John 24
Coldham, Tho. 12
Cole, Edward 29
  Gilbert 30
  Isaack 16
  Jno. 23, 29
  Jno., senr. 25
  Nicho. 23
  Wm. 23
Coleman, Jno. 28
  Noah 27
  Thomas 15
  Wm. 29, 31
Coles, Rise 12
  Robte 10, 11
Colimer, Isa. 20
Collens, John 21
Collier, Tho. 24
  Thom. 21
Collins, Benjamn. 40
  Edward 18
  Hen., jun. 27
  Henry 15, 33
  Henry, junr. 40 (2)
  Henry, senr. 35
  Joseph, senr. 35
  Peter 29
Collishawe, Willm 12
Colljer, Moses 22
Collocott, Richard 12
Colton, Ephrajm 32
  Georg 25
  Isaac 39
  John 39
  Tho. 32
Comes, John 38
Comins, Isaack 19
Con, Tho. 32
Conant, Roger 10 (2)
Conkling, Ananias 19
Connant, Exercise 24
Conney, Jno. 26
Conniball, John 38
Convers, James 27
  Josias 22
Converse, Edw. 10, 11
  Edwd. 34
  Sam. 25
Convrse., Allen 20
Cook, Noah 39
  Steeven 36
Cooke, Aron 14
  Elisha 28
  Goerg 25
  Goerge 14

  John 19
  Joseph 14, 25, 28
  Philip 21
  Rich.' 13
  Robrt. 18
  Stephen 29
  Walter 22, 24
Coole, Samll. 10, 11
Cooley, Eliakim 39
Coolidge, John 14
  Nath. 26
Cooly, Dani. 33
Cooper, John 15, 19
  Thom. 21
  Thomas 16, 39
Cop, David 27
  Willi. 18
Copie, James 18
Corbyn, Robert 24
Corlet, Eliiah 21
Corning, Samu. 18
Cornish, James 26
Corwin, George, Capt. 25
  John 25
  Jonothan 27
Cotte, Jno. 27
Cotton, Jno. 31
  John 12
  Seaborn 24
  Wm. 21
Cotty, Robte 14
Couch, Jno. 23
Courser, Will. 14
Courteous, Tho. 23
Cowels, John 38
Cowman, Richard 23
Cox, Richard 29
  Shadrick 29
  Tho. 29, 30
  Tho., jun. 29
  Thomas 29
  Wm. 29
Coxe, Robt. 26
Coytemore, Thoma. 17
Crabb, John 10
Crackborne, Gilbert 14
Craft, Sam. 27
Cranwell, John 10, 12
Crispe, Ben. 21
Crithley, Richrd. 19
Croad, Jno. 24
Crocket, Tho. 23
Crofte, Griffin 11
Cromwell, Phillip 25
Crosbee, Symon 26
Crosbey, Joseph 39
Crosby, Simon 14
Crosse, John 17
Croufot, Joseph 28
Crow, Jno. 26
Crowne, Wm., Colonell 24
Crumwell, Samll. 13
Cumings, Rich. 26
Cumins, Isa. 28
  Jno. 28
Cumpton, John 13
Cunley, Abraham 22
Curriar, Thomas 39
Curtis, Ephraim 34
  Goerge 18
  Henry 29
  Henry, jun. 29
  Samuel 39
  Theoph. 34
  Willm 11
Curtiss, John, Corpr. 36
Cushan, Thomas 38
Cushin, Dani. 28, 31

  Mathew, jun. 31
Cutler, Nath. 29
  Robrt. 15
Cutter, Richrd. 18
  William 15
Cuttin, Richard, senr. 37
Cutts, Rich. 25

--- D ---

D..., Danil. 32
Dady, Willm 12
Dallabar, Joseph, senr.
  33
Dalton, Tymo. 15
Dam, Jno. 28
Daming, John 20
Damman, Samuell 40
  Thomas 40
Dane, Danell 35
  Jno. 32 (2)
  Philemon 29
Danford, Samu. 21
Danforth, Jonath., juni.
  37
  Nich. 14
  Samu. 21
  Tho. 20
Daniel, Tho. 26
  Willi. 21
Dannell, Robert 16
Dants, Robrt. 20
Dare, Jno. 29
Darse, Benja. 34
Dassette, John 18
Dauson, Hen. 30
  Henry 18
Davenish, Thom. 18
Davenport, Charls 37
  Jno., jun. 36
  Jno., senr. 26
  Nathaniel 28
  Rich. 13
  Thom. 19
Davies, Daniell 23
  Geo. 21
  George 20
  Jenkin 15
  Samu. 20
  Thom. 18
  Willi. 20
Davis, Benja. 38 (2)
  James 13, 17, 25
  Jno. 23 (2), 26
  John 30, 36
  Joseph 25
  Niccolas 23
  Sam. 30
  Samuell 35
  Simon 35
  Simon, Lt. 36
  Tobias 26
  Wm. 28
Davy, Humphry 25
  John 14
Dawes, Wm. 21
Daws, Ambrose 27
Dawson, Henery 38
Day, James 28
  Mathew 21
  Ralph 21, 35
  Robte 13
  Thomas 26
  Thomas, junr. 39
  Timothy 35
Daye, Robrt. 18

Deane, Franses 39
    John 18
    Tho. 26, 28
Deering, Henry 26
Dell, Georg 22
Deming, Nicco. 29
Denison, Edwa. 21
    Georg 21
    William 36
Denlo, Wm. 29
Dennell, Tho. 23
Dennet, Jno. 28
Dennison, Danll. 12
    Willm 11
Denselow, Nich. 11
Dent, Frauncis 13
Devereux, Jno. 33
Devotion, Edwa. 21
Dewey, Tho. 12
Dewing, Andrew 21
Dewy, Jeddedia 31
Dexter, Tho. 11
Diamont, Jno. 22
Dibell, Robte 13
Dible, Thomas 15
Dickenson, Nathll., senr. 38
    Nehemiah 38
    Philemon 18
    Samll., senr. 38
Dickerman, Thomas 16
Dickinson, James 33
Dickson, Willi. 19
Dillingham, John 10, 11
Dimocke, Thom. 14
Dineley, Willi. 15
Dinny, Edward 15
    Will. 15
Dinsdale, Wm. 24
Diven, John 40
Dix, John 40
Dixe, Anthony 11
    Edward 13
    Ralfe 33
Dixie, Ralfe 34
Dixon, Wm. 23
Dixy, Willm 12
Dodg, John, junr. 39
    Richard 39
    Wm., jun. 33
Dodge, Edwd. 33
    Jno., jun. 33
    Jno., senr. 26
    Joseph 31
    William 15
Doggett, John 10, 11
Doley, Jno. 31
Dolling, John 29
Dolton, Philemon 14
Donell, Henry 23
Dorchester, James 39
    John 39
Dorman, Tho. 13
Dorr, Edwd. 24
Doryfall, Bernaby 14
Douglas, Henry 24
Douning, Dennis 23
Douse, Franc. 19
    Samuel 29
Dow, Hen. 26
    Henry 15
    Jno. 25
    Steven 26
Dowdy, Georg 21
Dowe, Thomas 19
Downeing, Emanuel 16
Downinge, Will. 38
Downton, Wm. 26

Dowse, Bengamin 36
    Jno. 30
    Law. 21
Drake, John 10
    Joseph 40
Drakenbury, Will. 10
Draper, Jams, senr. 36
    Richard 38
    Roger 16
Dressar, John 33
Dresser, Jno. 33
Drinker, Philip 15
Drury, Hugh 23
    John 28
Dryver, Robte 14
Dudley, Joseph 27
    Samu. 18
    Thom. 14
Duglas, Willi. 21
Dumer, Jerr. 31
    Rich. 11
    Richd., jun. 30
    Shubal 25
    Steven 16
    Thom. 17
Dun, Thom. 21
Duncan, Nathanaell 13
Dunnam, Nathaniell 35
Dunny, James 38
Dunster, Henry 18
Dunton, John 40
Durston, Tho. 22
Dussett, Jno. 24
Dwight, Tho. 22
    Timo. 24
    Tymo. 18
Dwisdsall, Tho. 24
Dwite, John 16
Dyar, George 10, 11
    Joseph 31
    Willm 14
Dyer, Benja. 30
    Joseph 32
    Tho. 30
    Thom. 20

--- E ---

Eales, John 12
Eames, Anthony 15
    Henry 33
    Tho. 25
East, Francs. 15
Eastman, Nathll. 37
Eastmond, John 38
Easton, Joseph 13
    Nicholas 13
Eastowe, William 16
Easty, Isack 28
Eaton, Dani. 34
    Jno. 30
    John 14, 40
    Jonas 22, 24, 40
    Jonathan 40
    Joseph 37
    Josh. 34
    Joshuah 40
    Natha. 16
    Tho. 26, 32
    William 40
    Wm. 22, 24
Eborne, Thomas 12
Eburne, Sam., sen. 25
Eckels, Richrd. 19
Ed..., Robt. 23
Eddenden, Edmo. 25

Eddington, Edmo. 25
Edey, Samll. 35
Edgcomb, Nico. 24
Edmnds, Robrt 29
Edmonds, Daniel 26
    John 11
    Joshua 22
    Saml. 35
    Walter 16
    Willm 14
Edmunds, John 40
    Robt. 29
Edwards, John 39
    Mathew 26
    Nathaniel 39
    Robrt. 19
    Thom. 19
    Wm. 29
Edwords, Joseph 39
    Samll. 39
Edy, John 13
Eggerly, Tho. 28
Egglestone, Bigatt 10
    Biggott 11
Eliot, Francis 18
Eliott, Jacob 23
Elis, John 18
Elistone, George 38
Elkines, Henry 13
Ellery, Wm. 28
Ellingham, Wm. 23
Ellings, Antho. 29
Elliot, Philip 14
Elliott, Jno. 24
Ellis, Jos. 24
Elljot, Andrew, jun. 33
Ellsley, John 17
Ellyott, Jacob 11
    John 11
Elsly, Wm. 33
Elson, Jno. 23
Elwell, Robert 17
Ely, Joseph 39
    Nathanaell 13
    Sam. 32
Elzie, Elisha 28
Emans, Tho. 22
Emerson, John, junr. 39
    Joseph 23
    Robert 26
Emery, Antho. 23
    James 22
    John 18
    John, junr. 39
    Jonathan 39
Emons, Benja. 30
Endecott, John 25
    Zerubbabl 25
Endicot, ---, Mr. 16
English, James 40
    Will. 19
Ensigne, James 13
Epps, Daniel 29
Esterbrooke, Joseph 25
Estman, Benjamin 37
    Samll. 37
Esty, Isa. 32
Evance, Hen. 21
Evans, Rich. 20
Eveleigh, Isaacke 34
Everad, Rich. 21
Evered, Andrew 23
Everett, Wm. 23
Everill, James 13
Everit, John 35
Everitt, Samll. 35
Evert, John 15
Evins, Richerd 37

Ewelle, Jose. 33
Ewer, Tho. 14
Eyers, John 38
Eyre, Symon 15

--- F ---

F..., Willi. 18
Fairbank, Jona. 35
  Joseph 31
Fairbanks, Joseph 33
Fairebancks, Richard 12
Fairefeild, John 17
Fairefield, Wm. 39
Faireweather, Jno. 28
Faireweathr., Tho. 12
Fairfeild, Dani. 33
Fairfield, Walter 39
Far, Benjamn. 40
  Jos. 32
Farewell, Henry 16
Farle, Caleb, senr. 37
Farnham, Jno. 27
Farnum, John 17
  Joseph 29
  Tho. 26
Farnworth, Joseph 16, 21
  Mathias 27
  Mathyas 27
Farr, George 14
  Joseph 35
Farrar, Thomas 35
  Thomas, junr. 40
Farrington, Jno. 26, 32
  Mathew, junr. 40
  Theophilus 40
  Willm. 40
Farwell, Jno. 32
Fasell, Jno. 23
Fawne, John 14
Faxon, Tho. 24
Fay, John 38
Feake, Robte 10
Feakes, Henry 13
  Robte 11
Feild, Alexandr. 21
  James 33
  John 38
  Robert 39
  Robrt. 20
Fellew, Abra. 24
Fellows, Joseph 32 (2)
  Sam. 20
Felows, Samll., junr. 37
Felpes, Willm. 11
Felton, Beniamin 16
  Jno. 32
Fering, Jno. 22
  John 30
Ferman, Gyles 12
  John 11
Ferrey, Charles 39
Ferris, Jeffery 13
  Zech. 30
Ferry, Charls 27
Fesenden, Nicholas 37
Filer, Walter 12
Fillipes, Nicho. 17
Fillips, Willi. 17
Finch, Abraham 13
  Danll. 11
  Samll. 12
Firman, Giles 16
  Josias 18
  Thomas 17
Firnam, Hen. 21

Fisher, Amos 35
  Antho. 20, 21
  Corneli. 22
  Daniell 18
  Danll. 35
  Jno. 32 (2)
  Josia 31
  Josiah 33
  Josua 18, 22
  Tho. 13, 29, 31
Fiske, David 15, 21, 34
  James 19
  Jno. 34
  John 15
  Moses 26
  Natha. 28
  Nathan 20
  Phineas 19
  Sam. 32
  Thos., junr. 39
  Willia. 19
  Wm. 27
Fisske, John 37
Fitch, Benja. 31
  Jeremiah 38
  Tho. 25
Fitche, Zachary 16
Fitt, Abraham 29
Flack, Cotten 18
Flackman, Thomas 18
Flag, Eliezer 36
Flagg, Gershom 29
Flanders, John 37
  Philip 37
Flecher, Samuell 35
Flecther, Joseph 37
Fleg, Beniamin 37
Flegg, Jno. 32
Fletcher, Edward 18
  Franc. 30
  Jnoo. 26
  Joshuah 35
  Samll. 35
  Will. 35
Fletchr., Willi. 20
Flint, Gorge 40
  John 36
  Joseph 36
  Thom. 15
  Thomas, Ensign 36
Flinte, Henry 14
Floyd, John 35
  Joseph 35
Flynt, Josiah 27
Fogg, Ralfe 13
Foored, Andrew 24
Foot, Isack 30
  John 39
Foote, Nathanell 13
Ford, Tho. 11
  Thomas 10
Formais, Mark 17
Fosdick, ---, Sargent 35
Fosditch, Steven 16
Fossenden, John 18
Foster, Andrew 26
  Andruw 39
  Christopher 15
  Edward 39
  Ely 35
  Hopestil 28
  Isack 27, 31
  James 31
  Jno. 32
  Jocob 34
  John 38
  Joseph 37
  Samll. 35

  Samuell 22
  Standfast 37
  Tho. 25
  Thom. 21
  Thoma. 19
  Wm. 30
Fostere, Hopestill 16
Foule, George 16
Fowkes, Henry 13
Fowlar, Thomas 39
Fowle, Isaack 30
  James 26
Fowler, Phillip 13
Fowlerer, Samll. 37
Fownell, John 21
Fox, Eliphelet 35
  Jabez 30
  Thom. 20
Foxe, Thom. 15
Foxewell, Rich. 11
  Willm Chase 10
Foxwell, Richard 24
  Frances, Richrd. 18
Francis, Stephen 35
Frary, Eliazr. 31
Frayrye, John 16
Freary, Jno. 24
Freathy, Wm. 23
Freeborne, Willm 13
Freeman, Jnothan. 33
  Jonath. 31
  Joseph 31
  Sam. 16
  Samll. 10
Freind, James 39
French, Jacob 22, 29, 30
  John 20
  Joseph 36
  Simon 37
  Steven 12, 32
  Tho. 11, 29
  Willm 14
Frie, James 39
Frissel, Jams 36
Frost, Charles 22
  Edmond 14
  Ephrai. 34
  Joseph 27
  Niccolas 22
  Sam. 31
  Samel. 37
Frothingham, Nath. 27
  Sam. 27
  Willm 11
Frothrington, Peter 26
Fry, George 22
  Jno. 26
Fuller, Benjamine 36
  Edward 40
  Jacob 36
  Jno., jun. 32
  Jnoth. 28
  Jnothan. 27, 32
  John 35
  John, senr. 36
  Joseph 32
  Joshua 32
  Robrt. 18
  Robt. 32
  Thom. 35
  Thomas, junr. 36
  Willi. 18
  Wm. 31
Furnell, Strong 20
Fyfield, Giles 27

48

--- G ---

Gage, Benj 26
Benj. 27
John 12
Josiah 33
Sam. 27
Gaildthait, Tho. 12
Gajle, Hugh 23
Gale, Benj. 36
Gallard, Will. 10
Gallerd, Willm 11
Gallop, John 12
Gallop, Samuel 24
Gally, John 27
Gamblin, Benjamin 36
Gamlyn, Robte. senr. 12
Gamlyne, Robte 13
Gamon, Robert 29
Gardiner, Jno. 31, 33
Josep 28
Rich. 22
Sam. 30
Sam., jun. 32
Gardner, Edmond 18
George 19
Peter 36
Thom. 15, 18
Gardnr., Thom. 21
Garey, Wm. 22
Garfield, Edward 13
Garfilld, Beniamin 37
Garfoard, Jarvas 17
Garnesey, Wm. 23
Garnsy, Henry 37
Garret, James 17
Garrett, Rich. 10
Gary, Sam. 26
Gate, Edmo. 25
Gates, Steeven 24
Gay, John 13, 20, 35
Jona. 35
Nathani. 30
Gaye, John 20
Gaynes, Henry 16
Geares, Willi. 18
Gearfield, Joseph 36
Gedney, John 15
Gee, Joshua 30
Geeree, Arthur 16
Genery, John 37
Lambrt. 20
Genings, Stephen 38
Gennison, Willm 11
George, Nicho., senr. 25
Gerrish, Benja. 32
John 27
Joseph 28, 29
Gibbins, Edw. 10
James 23
Gibbons, Edw. 11
Gibbs, Benja. 25
Gyles 11
Robert 24
Robt. 36
Gibson, Christopher 10
John 15
Samll. 37
W'm. 30
Giddings, Geo. 16
Joseph 32
Gidney, Barthol. 26
Eliazr. 27
Jno. 26
Gilbert, Jno. 32
Gill, Arthur 19
Jno. 25

Samll. 37
Tho., jun. 30
Gillett, Nath. 12
Gillom, Beniamyn 13
Gilman, Edwa. 20
Edward 16
Gingden, Jno. 29
Gingen, John 21
Ginner, Thomas 17
Gipson, John 27
Girdler, Francis 30
Gittings, Tho. 30
Glass, Richard 29
Glover, Charles 18
Habbacuck 22
Nath. 23, 31
Ralfe 10
Goard, Rich. 20
Gobile, Thomas 35
Goble, Thomas 13
Godard, Willyam 37
Godfree, Willi. 17
Godfry, Edward 23
Goffe, Edward 14
Jno. 30
Gold, Jno. 25
Robt. 31
Goldsmith, Zackeus 34
Gooch, Jno. 23
Goodale, Zechariah, senr. 36
Goodenew, Samuell 38
Goodenow, John 28
Goodhewe, Will. 14
Goodhue, Joseph 29
Wm., jun. 32
Goodin, Xtopher 30
Gooding, Edward 19
Nath. 31
Goodman, John 38
Rich. 12
Goodnor, Edmond 17
Goodnow, John 18
Thom. 20
Goodwin, John 30
Willm 11
Gooffe, John 16
Gookens, Dan., Cap. 20
Gookin, Dani., jun. 30
Samuell 37
Gooldsmith, Zecheas 39
Goose, Isaac 38
Gore, John 15
Samuel 36
Gorton, Jno. 26
Gosse, John 11
Got, Charl 32
Gott, Charles 10 (2), 24
Dani. 27
Gouen, Nathanell 40
Gould, John 16
Nathan 39
Thom. 18
Gowing, Robrt. 20
Grafton, Jno. 31
Joseph 15, 26
Grant, Edw. 27
Math. 11
Graves, Isack 26
Jno. 34
John 15
Samull. 40
Tho. 10 (2)
Thoma. 17
Thomas 28
Thomas, senr. 40
Green, James 21, 33
Jno. 26

John 33, 35
Samuell 35
Tho. 27 (2)
Thomas 35
Willi. 20
Greene, ---, Srieant 12
Bartholmewe 12
Henry 17
Jacob 22
James 38
Jno. 22, 23
John 19, 38
Nath. 25
Natha. 21
Passevell 14
Samll. 13
Wm. 26
Greenehill, Samll. 13
Greenland, Jno. 31
Greenleaf, Steph. 30
Greenliffe, Edmond 16
Greenore, Wm., jun. 28
Greenough, Wm. 26
Greenwood, Thomas 36
Grele, Andrew 37
Philip 37
Grene, Isaac 37
Gridley, Rich. 12
Griffin, Hugh 20
Griffinn, Richrd. 15
Griffyn, Rich. 24
Griggs, John 36
Jos. 22
Joseph 24
Wm. 28
Grimes, Samu. 19
Grinnoway, John 11
Grinoway, John 10
Grise, Charles 22
Josiah 38
Samll. 38
Grissell, Franc. 21
Grout, Jno. 25
Grover, Edmo. 31
Lazurus 35
Nehem. 31
Simon 35
Thomas 35
Grubb, Thomas 12
Guil, Samu. 19
Guile, Abra. 32
John 20
Sam. 31
Gull, Wm. 28
Gullifer, Antho. 25
Gun, Jasper 14
Tho. 13
Gunison, Hugh 22
Gunlithe, Henry 20
Gunn, Tho. 26
Gunnison, Hugh 14
Guppee, Jno. 22, 24
Gurnell, John 20
Gurney, Richd. 32
Gutch, Robrt. 19
Guttering, John 19
Guye, Nichol. 16
Gyles, Edw. 12

--- H ---

Habersfeild, ---, Mr. 40
Habord, Johnethen 35
Hackburne, Abra. 20
Samu. 15
Hadden, Jerad 12

Hollister, John 20 (2)
Holman, Abr. 24
  Tho. 31
Holmes, George 17
  Joseph 38
  Robrt. 18
Holt, Nicolas 15
Holton, Jno. 27
  Joseph, junr. 36
  Joseph, senr. 36
  Ralph 26
  Samll. 39
  Wm. 33
Homan, Samll. 35
Hood, Richard 40
  Richd., senr. 40
Hooke, Will. 37
  Willi. 18
Hooker, Tho. 12
Hoole, Tho. 25
Hooper, Wm. 21
Hoord, Jno. 22
Hopkins, John 13
Hopkinson, Micha. 17
Horne, John 10
Horrel, Humphry 33
Horseford, Willm 12
Hort, Joseph 40
  Samll. 40
Hosier, Samll. 10, 11
Hoskins, John 10, 11, 12
  Thomas 13
Hosmer, Steven 36
  Tho. 13
Hough, Atterton 12
Houlden, Justinian 24
Hoult, Samuel 39
Houlton, Robte 12
Hovey, Daniell 29
  Tho. 32
How, Eliazer 38
  Isaac 36 (2)
  Isace 37
  Israel 31
  James 26
  Jno. 34
  Joseph 24
  Sam. 27
  Samuel 36
  Thomas 37
Howard, John 36
  Nathaniell 35
  Robrt. 33
  Robt. 22
Howchenes, Jeremy 17
Howe, Abraham 15
  Danll. 12
  Edw. 12
  Edward 15
  James 15
  John 17
Howell, Edward 16
  Morgan 23
Howen, Robert 19
Howlett, Tho. 12
Howman, John 10
Howrd., Nathani. 20
Hoytt, Simon 11
Hubard, Caleb 27
  Richard 37
Hubbard, Beniamin 13
  Danl. 38
  Edmond 13
  Enock 31
  James 25
  Jerremiah 22
  Jerremy 24
  Jno. 30, 33

  Joshua 22, 24
  Josiah 24
  Josuah 13
  Neh. 31
  Rich. 26
  Tho. 12
  Wm. 22, 24
Hubbart, David 32
Hubberd, William 16
Hubbert, Edmond 12
  Peter 14
  Samll. 13
Huchison, Frances 40
Hudson, Francis 28
  Jonathan 40
  Moses 40
  Nicolas 15
  Ralph 14
  Willi. 18
  Willm 11
Huit, Thom. 21
Hulberd, Willm 10
Hulbert, Willm 11
Hull, George 11
  John 11, 22
  Joseph 14
  Rich. 12
  Robert 15
  Thomas 39
Hulling, --- 16
Humber, Edw. 25
Humfrey, John 14
Humphreys, Thomas 29
Humphry, Hopstill 37
  Isack 37
  Jonas 22, 24
  Nath 31
  Sam. 31
Humphryes, Jonas 17
Hund, Zach. 31
Hunn, George 15
Hunt, Ephraim 27
  Jonathan 31
  Nemiah 35
  Sam. 23
  Samuel 36
  Tho. 33
  Willi. 18
Hunter, Robrt. 18
Hunting, John 16, 35
Hurd, Jacob 31
  John 18
Hurryman, Leonard 24
Huse, Edward 35
Hussey, Christopher 12
  Robert 38
Hutchingson, Edw. 12, 13
  Fr. 13
  George 12
  Rich. 13
  Will. 13
Hutchins, Rich. 10
  Wm. 33
Hutchinson, Eljakim 28
  Frans. 34
  Joseph, senr. 36
  Nath. 24
Huthinson, Elish. 26
Hutton, Rich. 28

    --- I ---

Ingalls, Hen. 28
  Henry 29
Ingersoll, Jno. 26
  Nathanael 36

Ingoldsbey, John 19
Ingolls, Robt. 40
  Sam. 32
  Samuell 40
  Tho. 27
Ingols, John, senr. 40
Ingram, Jno. 33
  Wm. 29
Ireland, Wm. 22
Isaack, Joseph 15
Islin, Thom. 17
Ives, Mathias 14

    --- J ---

Jackewish, Abr. 24
Jackline, Samuell 38
Jacklinge, Edmonde 13
Jackman, James 33
Jackson, Abraham 36
  Edmond 14
  Edwa. 20
  Edwd. 34
  Jno. 29
  John 18, 20, 30
  Jonathan 27
  Seabis 36
  Thomas 38
Jaco, Eljazer 27
Jacob, Jos. 32
  Nath. 33
  Nicholas 14
  Richard 14
  Tho. 29
Jacquish, Henry 26 (2)
Jakson, Edward 36
James, Edmond 10
  Franc. 20
  Francs 33
  Gawdy 19
  Tho. 11
  Wating 33
  Willm 10
Jarrat, John 17
Jcques, Steaphen 39
Jeffries, Will. 10
Jeffry, Tho. 12
  Willm 11
Jefts, Henry, juni. 37
Jellett, Jonathan 13
Jeningson, Sam. 32
Jenison, Robrt. 21
Jenkin, Reignald 23
Jenkins, Joel 21
  Obadia 35
Jenner, David 40
  Thom. 14
Jennison, Willm 10
Jeofferjes, Gregory 23
Jewet, Ezek. 26
  Ezekiel 28
  Jno. 30 (2)
  Joseph 17, 33
  Maxami. 17
  Nehemiah 26
Jewett, Nath. 32
Jincks, Rich. 33
Joanes, James 20
  John, stud. 20
  Tho. 21
  Thom. 16
Joans, Daved 37
Jocelyn, Henry 24
Johnson, ---, Cornet 40
  Davy 11
  Ebenezr. 33

Lion, Peeter 37
Lipincote, Richrd. 17
Lister, Andrew 20
Litlefeild, Antho. 23
  Frauncis, jun. 23
  Frauncis, senr. 23
  Tho. 23
Livermore, John 36
  Sam. 27
Lobdell, Isack 28
  Jno. 28
Lockewood, Edmond 11
Lockwood, Edmond 10
  Robrt. 15
Longe, Robrt. 14, 21
Looker, Henry 20
  John 21
Lord, Nath. 22
  Rich. 13
  Robte 14
  William 17
Loreing, Tho. 14
Loring, Benj. 28
  Jno. 28
  Tho. 28
Louden, Jno. 26
Lovejoy, Jno. 28
  John 29
Lovell, Robte 14
Loverin, John 14
Lovet, Danel 29
Lovioy, Joseph 39
  William 39
Lowden, Richrd. 19
Lowell, Benja. 26
  John 18
Lowthrop, Tho. 12
Ludkin, George 14
  Willi. 15
Ludlowe, George 10
Luise, John 33
Lull, Tho. 28
Lumbard, David 39
Lumberd, Tho. 10, 11
Lumbert, Bernard 12
Lumkin, Richrd. 16
Lumpson, Jno. 29
Lunt, Dani. 33
  Henry 16
  John 29
Lussher, Eleazer 16
Luxford, Ruben 29, 30
Lydget, Peter 28
Lyman, Rich. 12
Lymon, Robt. 33
Lyncoln, Josh. 27
Lynd, Joseph 27
  Thomas 13
Lyndall, Timo. 30
Lynds, John 31
  Joseph 31
Lynzey, Jno. 35
Lynzy, Eleazer 40
Lyon, Georg 26
  John 36
  Joseph 31
  Peter 22
  Wm. 25
Lytlefeild, Jno. 27

--- M ---

Maddock, Henry 23
Mader, Robrt. 20
Madinde, Mich. 24
Maggott, Joseph 13

Mahewe, Tho. 12
Maies, John 18
Mainerd, John, senr. 37
Maisters, John 11
Majes, Jno. 24
  Sam. 24
Man, Sam. 31
Mang, Georg 25
Maning, Samuell 27
Manley, William 38
Manning, Willi. 18, 20
Mansfeild, Andrew 40
  Daniell 40
  Jno. 33
  John 20
  Joseph, junr. 40 (2)
Marble, Wm. 24
March, Georg 33
  John 19
Marcham, Nath. 32
Markeham, Dani. 30
Markham, Daniel 29
Marret, Jno. 25
Marrion, Jno. 31
Marrjon, Jo. 22
Marryott, Tho. 14
Marsh, Alex. 23
  Daniall 38
  Jonathan 38
  Onesepherus 28
  Samll. 38
  Tho. 23, 31
  Zache 31
  Zacke 40
Marshal, Samll. 39
Marshall, Edmond 15
  Jno. 27, 33
  John 37, 38
  Samll. 40
  Samuell 35
  Rho. 13, 22
  Thom. 19, 20
  Thomas 13, 24
Marshe, George 14
Marshell, Edward 35
Marshfield, Josias 39
Marston, Jno. 27
  John 18
  Manasses 30
  Thom. 18
  Wm. 26
Marten, Robrt. 17
  Thomas 16
Martial, Christ. 13
Martin, Jno 25
  John 17
Martine, Thomas 38
Martjn, Jno. 26
  Solomon 22
  Wm. 22
Martyn, Rich. 24
  Wm. 24
Mascoll, Jno. 30
Masie, Thomas 17
Maskor, Jno. 27
Mason, Arthur 24
  Henry 22
  Hugh 13
  John 36
  John, Capt. 13
  Joseph 35
  Robert 28
  Sam 26
  Thomas 27
Massey, Jno. 26
Massy, Jeffery 12
Maston, John, senr. 39
Mather, Cotton 31

  Sam. 21
  Wareham 39
Mathis, John 19
Matson, Tho. 12
  Tho., jun. 25
Mattocke, David 22
Mattoone, Hugbert 22
Mattucke, James 16
Maude, Daniel 14
Maudsley, Jno. 31
  John 16
Mavericke, Antipas 23
  Elias 38
Mavracke., Elias 12
  John 10 (2)
  Moses 13
  Samll. 10
Mavricke, Samll. 11
Mawry, Roger 11
Maxwell, Jno. 26
May, Georg 25
  John 36
Maynard, Jno., senr. 34
  John 20, 21
Meade, Gabriell 15
  Ri. 25
Meads, David 33
Meakins, Thomas 15
Medcalfe, Micha. 21
  Mychall 18
  Tho. 22, 24
MedCalfe, Jonathan 33
Mekyn, Thom., junior 14
Melby, Nath. 31
Mellen, Richrd. 17
Mellowes, Abraham 12
  Edw. 12
  Jno. 27
  Ollyver 13
Mendam, Robt. 22
Meriam, Joseph 40
Merriam, George 19
  Jno. 30
  Joseph 16
  Robert 16
  Will. 22
  Willm. 40
Merrick, Thomas 25
Merril, Daniel 33
Merrill, Danel 33
  John 17
Merrit, Jno. 33
Merrow, Henry 30
Merry, Walter 12
Messenger, Hen. 25
Metcalf, Michael 35
  Tho. 29
Metcalfe, Jnothan. 33
  John 21
  Joseph 13
  Micha. 19
Michell, Jona. 21
Middlecott, Richd. 38 (2)
Mighill, Thoma. 17
Mile, Joseph 23
Miles, Benj. 31
  John 16
  Sam. 20
Millar, James 30
  Jose. 34
Miller, Alexander 15
  John 17, 39
  Samuel 39
  William, senr. 39
Milles, Tho. 23
Millet, Thomas 15
Millett, Rich. 12
Mills, John 10

53

Minerd, Jams 35
Mingy, Jeffry 17
Minor, Thomas 12
Minot, Gorg 37
  James 25
  Jno. 25
  John 37
  Stephen 25
Minott, George 12
Miriam, John 21
Mirock, Jno. 34
Mirriam, Joseph 22
Mirricke, John 39
Mitten, Mich. 24
Mixer, Isaack 15
Modsley, Hen. 21
Mondy, Danell 37
Montague, Peter 38
Moody, Caleb 25
  Eleazer 38
  John 12
  Sam. 25
  Willm 13
  Wm. 33
Moor, Jno. 26
  John 40
Moore, Francis 22
  Jno. 25, 27
  John 11 (2)
  Richard 23
  Saml. 11
  Tho. 11, 36
  Wm. 23
Moores, Jonathan, Cornet
  39
Moors, Samuell 40
More, Francis 16
  Goulden 18
  Jeremy 20
  John 15
  Rich. 19
  Thom. 19
Morgan, David 39
  James 20
  Jonatha. 39
Morly, John 20
Morrall, Isaack 11
Morrel, Moses 39
Morrell, Isack 32
  Jacob 37
Morris, ---, Srieant. 10
Morriss, Isaac 36
Morse, Benja. 28
  Danll. 13
  Ezra 27
  Jno. 27, 28
  Jnoth. 30
  Jnothan. 27
  Jnothn. 27, 28
  John 23
  Joseph 13, 27, 28
  Obadiah 28, 29, 30
  Samu. 18
Morton, Charles 38
  Richd., senr. 38
Mory, Thomas 34
Mose, John 18
Mosse, Anthony 14
  Jno. 26
  Willm 14
Mott, Adam 14
Moulton, James 15
  John 16
  Robte 11
  Thom. 16
Mountague, Griffin 23
  Richd. 31
Mousell, John 13, 22

Moxam, George 15
Mudg, John 36
Mudget, Tho. 37
Munday, Henry 17
Munings, George 13
Munioy, George 21
Munroe, William 37
Mushell, Ralfe 10, 11
Mussellwhit, John 16
Mussey, Robte 13
Muste, Edw. 12
Muzzey, Benj. 25
Mylam, John 14
Myllett, Rich. 10
Mylls, John 11
Myriam, John 36
  Samuel 36

--- N ---

Nash, Jacob 26, 34
  James 20, 26
  Timo. 31
Nashe, Willm 13
Nason, Richard 22
Neale, Franc. 24
  John 19
Needam, Wm. 21
Needham, Daniell 40
Neges, Jabes 40
Negos, Jonathan 13
Negus, Benia. 21 (2)
Nelson, Phillip 25
  Tho. 25
  Thom. 17
Nethrland., Willm 13
Newall, Thomas 35
Newberry, Rich. 20
Newbery, Tho. 13
  Tryall 36
Newegate, John 13
Newel, Jacob 36
  John 36
Newell, Abra. 22, 24
  Abraham 13
Neweman, Samuel 16
Neweton, John 11
Newhall, Jno. 33
  John, Ensign 40
  John, senr. 40
  Joseph 35
  Nathan, junr. 40
  Nathaniell, senr. 40
Newton, Antho. 27
  John 20
  Josep. 34
  Joseph, senr. 40
  Rich. 20, 21
Newtten, John 37
  Moses 38
Niccolls, Adam 27
Nicholate, Charls 28
Nicholes, John 38
Nicholls, Ephrm. 33
  James 26
Nichols, Tho. 33
Nickerson, Willi. 15
Nickols, James 40
  John 40
  Thomas 40
Nicoles, Walter 14
Nightingall, William,
  junr. 39
Nile, Jonathan 31
Noble, Tho. 32
Noddle, Willm 11

Nogget, Sam. 33
Noise, James 13
  Nicolas 15
Norcros, Natha. 20
Norcross, --- 22
Norcrosse, Ric. 22
Norden, Nathll., Capt. 36
  Sam. 25, 26
Norman, Richd. 31
  Tho. 32
Norrice, Edwar. 17
North, Richrd. 18
Norton, Francis 19
  Georg 32
  George 12
  Henry 23
  John 15
  Waltr., Capt. 10 (2)
  Willm 14
Norwick, John 17
Nowel, Sam. 30
Nowell, Alexandr. 27
  Increase 14
Noyce, Peter 28
Noyes, Cutting 29
  Jno. 29, 30
  Tho. 27
Noys, Tymothy 33
Noyse, Peter 17
Nurs, Frances, senr. 36
Nurse, Samuel 36
Nutte, Myles 15
Nutter, Antho. 26
Nutting, John 24
Nyles, John 21

--- O ---

Oake, Samll. 38
Oakeman, Samuell 24
Oakes, Urian 27
Oaks, Thomas 35
Odlyn, John 12
Okes, Edward 19
  Thom. 19
Oldam, John 37
  Samuell 28
Oldeham, John 11
Oldum, Samuell 36
Oliver, James 18
  John 17
  Nathaniel 38
  Peter 18
Olliver, Daniell 38
  David 29
  James 38
  Jno. 32
  John 33
  Natha. 38
  Richard 29
Ollivr., Tho. 28
Ollyver, John 12
  Tho. 11
Olmstead, James 11
Olney, Thom. 15
Onion, Robrt. 21
Ordaway, James 26
Osborne, John 28
  Willi. 17
Osbourne, Nicho. 29
Osburn, William 36
Osburne, Thom. 21
Osgood, Christ. 14
  John 16
  John, junr. 39
  Steven 26

Tho. 30
Timothy 39
Will. 37
Xtopher 30
Osmer, James 15
Ottis, John 14
Ouldam, Rich. 22
Overmore, Tho. 27
Owen, Wm. 22
Oxenbridge, Jno. 27

--- P ---

Paddeshall, Rich. 28
Paffer, Robert, senr. 40
Page, Hen. 25
    John 10, 11, 18
    Nath. 37
    Robrt. 19
Pain, Philip 39
Paine, Robrt. 18
    Steven 17
    Willi. 17
Painter, Thomas 18
Pajne; Robrt., jun. 34
    Steeven 22, 24
    Stephen 25
    Wm. 22
Palfry, Peter 10
    Petr. 11
Palgrave, Rich. 10, 11
Palmer, Abraham 10, 11
    Henry 19, 29
    Jno., jun. 29
    Jno., senr. 29
    John 16, 18
    Sam. 33
    Samll. 33
    Waltr. 11
    William 16
    Wm. 22
Pannly, Alex. 24
Pantry, Willm 13
Pardon, Willi. 20
Parish, Thomas 15
Park, Jacob 24
Parke, Tho., senr. 32
Parkeman, Elias 13
Parker, Abr. 20, 32
    Abrah. 35
    George 23
    Hananiah 31
    Jacob 35
    James 12
    Jno. 23 (2), 29, 31
    John 22, 40
    Nathanell 40
    Nich. 12
    Richrd. 18
    Robte 13
    Tho. 13, 29
    Thomas 15
    Willi. 18
Parkes, Tho. 27
Parkhurst, Geo. 20
Parkhust, John 37
Parkr., James 20
Parks, Willm 11
Parmenter, John 17, 20
Parmiter, Benj. 30
    Jos. 31
    Robt 22
Parnell, Tho. 29
Parr, Abell 18
Parrat, Franc. 17
Parris, Sam. 33

Parsons, James 33
    Jona. 33
    Joseph 26, 38
    Robert 16
    Samuel 39
    Wm. 21
Partridge, Natha. 20
    Willi. 16
Pary, Wm. 21
Pason, Edw. 31, 32
    Ephraim 37
    Ephraj. 34
    Gyles 15
    John 31
    Samuel 37
Passens, Jephrey 35
    John 35
Passon, Edwrd. 17
Patch, Jno. 31
    Ric. 31
    Tho. 27
Patridg, Wm. 22
Patridge, Wm. 24
Patten, Nathaniel 30
    Tho. 31
    Willi. 21
Pattestall, Edmnd, Capt.
    29
Pattinggell, Richrd. 18
Pattison, James 37
Pattricke, Danll., Capt.
    10
Paule, Daniel 22
Payn, Samuel 39
Payne, Moses 18, 21
    Steph., jun. 31
    Thom. 18
Payson, Samuel 36
Peach, Jno., jun. 33
Peake, Christopher 13
    Jonathan 36
Pearce, John 15
    Richard, jun. 29
Pearley, Allen 19
Pearly, John 36, 39
    Tho. 30
Pearse, Beniamin 37
    Dani. 24
    Robt. 22
Pease, Henry 13
    Jno. 26
Peaseley, Joseph 19
Pebody, Franc. 19
    Jno. 29
    Joseph 39
    Wm. 34
Peck, Joseph 16
    Robert 16
Pecocke, Richrd. 17
Peelsbury, Wm. 26
Peerce, John 21
Peirce, Anthony 13
    Daniell 16
    John 11, 37
    Joseph 33
    Joseph, senr. 37
    Nathaniel 29
    Robert 19
    Sam. 27
    Samll. 33
    Tho. 13
    Willm 12
Peirse, Math. 34
    Tho. 25
Peirson, John 21
    Sam. 32
Pelham, Herbrt. 20
    Willm 10

Pell, Joseph 16
    Willm 13
Pellet, Daniel 36
    Thomas 36
Pemberton, Benjamen 38
    James 21
Pembrton., James 10
Pemerton, John 12
Peñ, James 10
Pendleton, Bryan 13
Pengilley, Jno. 31
Peniman, Jos. 31
Penniman, Jno. 27
    Sam. 31
Pennyman, James 11
Penticus, John 17
Pepper, Rich. 13
    Robrt. 20
Perkins, Abra. 17
    Isaack 19
    John 11, 15
    Tho, jun. 34
    Timothy 36
    Tobyah 34
    William 36
    Willm 13
Perkis, Joseph 35
Perly, Sam. 26
Perram, John 36
Perrum, Jno. 35
Perry, Arthur 17
    Isaack 11
    John 11
    Obadia 31
    Samuel 36
    Seth 25
Person, John 39
    Joseph 30
Peters, Hugh 14
Phelabrowne, Tho. 25
Phelpes, George 14
    Willm 10
Phelph, Nath. 32
Phelps, Edward 39
    Isack 27
    William 39
Phese, Willi. 20
Philbrick, Tho. 26
Philebrowne, Tho. 26
Philips, Tim. 38
Phillips, Eleazr. 35
    George 10 (2), 11
    Henry 16
    Jno. 30
    John 11, 24
    Rich. 31
    Tho. 29 (2)
    Walter, senr. 36
    Wm. 29
Phippen, Jos. 20, 32
Phippin, David 14
Phipps, Sollomon, jun. 27
    William, Sir, Knt. 34
    William, Sr. 38
Phips, Solomon 19
Pickard, Jno., jun. 33
Pickering, Jno. 26
Pid, Richrd. 19
Pidg, John 35
Pierce, Tho. 30
Pierpoint, Robt. 30
Pier Point, Jno. 22
Pierson, Jno., jun. 32
Pigg, Tho. 12
Pike, James 21
    Jno. 30
    Robert 15
    Robt., jr. 37

Pillips, John 10
Pilsbury, Job 27
  Moses 28
Pinchen, Willi. 19
Pinney, Tho. 28
Pinor, Jno. 32
Pitcher, Andrew 18
  Sam. 33
Pitman, Jno., Capt. 36
  Tho., senr. 33
Pitts, Edmo. 17
Pitty, Joseph 31, 32
Place, Peter 21
  Thom. 18
Platt, Samuel 33
Plumer, Frauncis 12
  Joseph 27
  Samu. 18
Plumr., Silvanus 39
Plunton, John 20
Poget, Tho. 21
Point, Jno. Pier 22
Pole, John 28
Pomrey, Joshua 31
Pomry, Joseph 31
Pond, Danll. 35
  Robert 19
Poore, John, jun. 27
  Sam. 28
Pope, John 13
  Joseph 15, 36
Porsune, Bartho. 21
Porter, Abell, jun. 28
  Edward 15
  Hezekiah 38
  Israel, jun. 34
  Israell 36
  John 12, 38, 39
  Jonathan 18
  Joseph 25
  Nathani. 15
  Rich. 24
  Richard 22
  Roger 17
  Sam. 34
  Steven 39
Portmorte, Philemon 13
Poster, Abell 29
Poter, Judath 35
Potter, Luke 16
  Robt., junr. 40
  Robte 13
  Willi. 18
Powell, Michaell 18
Powning, Hen. 20
Prat, Joseph 28
  Mathewe 17
  Thom. 21
Pratt, Abraham 10
  John 12, 20
  Joseph 29
  Sam. 25
  Timo. 33
  Wm. 22, 31
Preble, Abra. 23
Prence, Richrd. 19
Prentice, Henry 22, 34
  Tho. 22
  Tho., jun. 32
  Tho., senr. 32
  Valentine 11
Prentis, James, senr. 36
Prescot, Jno. 31
  Jonas 31
  Jonathan, Lt. 36
  Peter 32
Prescott, Jno. 26
Prest, James 20 (2)

Preston, Dani. 25
  Daniel 37
  Thomas 36
Price, David 14
  Jno. 30
  Richard 24
  Walter 19
Prichard, Hugh 19
Pride, John 29
Prince, John 13
  Sam. 31
  Samuel 31
Pritchard, Roger 21
Pritchet, John 34
Procter, Richard 38
Proctor, George 15
  John 38
  Robrt. 20
Prout, Ebenezar 38
  Ebenr. 34
  Joseph 38
  Tymo. 20
Pumbrey, Caleb 29
Pummery, Eltweed 11
Pumrey, Medad 27
Purchase, Oliver 14
Purkins, Abra. 34
Purrington, Robt. 28
Putman, Benja. 36
  Edward 36
  James 36
  Jno. 25
  John, secundus 36
  Jonathan 36
  Thom. 19
  Tho., jun. 31
Pynchon, John 21
Pyne, Thomas 13
Pynny, Humfry 12

——— Q ———

Quinsey, Daniell 38
  Edmo. 25
  Edmond 12

——— R ———

Raiment, Wm., jun. 33
Raines, Frauncis 23
Rainsfoard, Edward 15
Ramsdell, Aquilla 40
Rand, Jno. 28
  Nathani 26
  Robt., junr. 40
  Tho. 24
Randill, Phillipp 12
Randol, John 40
  Thomas 40
Ranger, Edmo. 27
Ravensdale, John 14
Rawlen, Rich. 20
Rawling, Jespr. 12
Rawlins, Tho. 11
  Thomas 10
Rawlinson, Thomas 16
Rawlyns, James 12
  Jespr. 13
  Tho. 14
Rawson, Edward 15
  Grindall 33
Ray, Tho. 33
Rayment, Jno. 33
  Thomas 36

Raymond, Rich. 12
Rayner, Wm. 27
Rea, Joshua 25
  Joshua, junr. 36
Read, Edw. 30
  Georg 33
  John 18
  Phillip 24
  Samuel 29
  Tho. 24
  Wm. 32
Reade, Esdras 18
  Tho., jun. 31
  Thomas 12
  Willm 14
  Wm. 22, 24
Reading, Thomas 23
Reads, Joseph 32
  Josiah 32
Reddin, Myles 12
Reddings, Joseph 12
Reddington, Dani. 34
Redington, Abraham 36
  Thomas 36
Rednap, Benjamn. 40
Rednape, Joseph 13
Reed, Georg 37
  William 16
Reeves, Thom. 21
Remeth, Christian 22
Rendell, Robrt. 21
Renolls, Wm. 23
Reynolds, Nath. 25
Reynolls, John 13
  Robert 13
Reynr., Humphrey 19
Rhoades, Joseph 35
Rhoads, Josiah 35
Rhodes, Josiah 40
  Samull. 40
Riall, Isack 37
Rice, Edmond 17
  Henry 21
  Joseph 28
  Joshua 38
  Mathew 24
  Richrd. 19
  Tho. 24
Richards, James 22
  Jno. 27, 32
  John 40
  Joseph 32
  Nath. 11, 35
  Thom. 20
  Wm., jun. 32
Richardson, Amos 25
  Ezekiell 11
  Jno. 31
  Joseph 28
  Josias 29
  Nathll. 37
  Steven 37
Richds., Jno. 31
Richrds., Edward 18
  Thom. 17
Richrdson., Samuell 15
  Thomas 15
Riddan, Thadeus 28
Rider, Tho. 35
Ries, Timothy 35
Riff, Richard 30
Rigbey, John 19
Riggs, Edward 12
Right, George 19
  Joseph, junr. 37
Riley, Jno. 27
Rimington, John 16
Rimgton, Tho. 28

Ringe, Jarvis 37
  Robrt. 18
Ripley, Abr. 24
  Jno. 24
  Willi. 19
Rise, Edward 22
Roads, John 33
  Joseph 30, 33
Roaper, John 18
Robbins, Nathaniell 36
  Sam. 31
  Samuell 36
  William 40
Robbinson, Nath. 28
Roberts, Jno. 26, 27
  Tho. 26
  Thom. 21
Robinson, Franc. 27
  James 37
  John 18
  Joseph 39
  Richrd. 18
  Samuel 37
  Willi. 19 (2)
  Wm. 34
Robrt., John 17
Rocke, Joseph 22
Rocket, Nicho. 25
Rockewell, Will. 10
  Willm 11
Rockwood, Sam. 32
  Samuel 32
Rodes, Theoph. 33
Rodgers, John 29
Roffe, John 17
Rogers, Ezechi. 17
  Jno. 27, 30, 37
  John 15, 16
  Natha. 16, 17
  Symon 17
  Thom. 15
  Thomas 23
  Wm. 23
Roise, Robte 12
Rolfe, Benj. 27
  Benja. 26
Root, Hezekiah 39
  Jacob 33
  Jonathan 39
Roote, Jno. 26
  Jose. 33
  Sam. 31
Roots, Richrd. 15
Ropper, Walter 19
Rossen, William 37
Rossiter, Bray 11
Rouse, Faithfull 20
Row, Jno. 28
Rowes, George 18
Ruck, Samuel 33
  Thom. 17
Rucke, Jno. 25
  Samuell, senr. 38
Ruddyk, John 17
Rugg, Jno. 26
Ruggles, George 12
  Jno. 24
  John 11, 15
  John, 2d. 36
  Thomas 16
Rugles, Jno. 23
  Jno., senr. 29
Rush, Jasper 20
Rushworth, Edward 23
Russe, John 39
Russell, Dani. 30
  Georg, Esq. 31
  James 26

James 26
Jno. 31
John 14, 20
Phillip 25
Richrd. 18
Robberd 39
Tho. 30
Russells, Jno. 32
Rust, Henry 15
  Israell 39
  Nathan. 29
Ruth, Vincent 21
Ryall, Wm. 31
Rydeat, John 21

--- S ---

Sadler, Anthony 17
  John 19
  Richrd. 16
Safford, Joseph 32
Saffyn, Jno. 27
Sajle, Obadiah 32
Sale, Edwa. 15
Sally, Manus 21
Salter, Will. 14
Saltonstal, Nath. 25
Saltonstall, Rich. 11
Samborne, Jno. 26
Samfoard, Thomas 15
Sampeford, John 11
Sampson, Richard 29
Sandford, John 27
Sandrbant., John 20
Sands, Henry 18
Sanford, Richrd. 18
Sanforth, Robt. 22
Sanyde, Jno. 32
Saretell, Thom. 21
Sargent, John 35
  Joseph 35
Sarjant, Thomas 39
Saunders, Jno. 23
  John 14, 17, 22
  Martjn 22
  Robert 17
Saunderson, Robert 17
Saundrs., Martin 18
Sautell, Jnothn. 27
Savage, Abijah 25
  Ephraim 27
  Tho., Major 38
  Thom. 14
  Thomas 38
  Thomas, Capt. 38
Savil, Jno. 34
  Sam. 34
Sawen, Jno. 22
Sawer, Tho. 23
Sawyer, Joshua 37
Says, Thomas 16
Saywell, David 26
Scadlocke, Willjam 23
Scales, Willi. 17
Scarbrow, Jno. 18
Scarlet, Sam., Capt. 28
Scot, John 36
Scott, Benja. 25
  John 36
  Peter 34
  Thomas 13
Scotte, Robert 14
Scotto, Thomas 16
Scraggs, Thomas 14
Seajles, James 33
Search, John 19

Searl, Ephraim 28
Seavir, Wm 29
Seawall, Henry, junrior
  15
  Sam. 30
Sebley, John 13
Sedgwick, Robert 15
Seely, Robte 10, 11
Seir, John 18
Selman, Jno. 29
Selsbe, Jonth. 33
Selsbee, Jonaathan 35
Sendall, Sam. 21
Senden, Sam. 33
Sension, Matthias 13
Seorls, John 39
Sergeant, Peter 38 (2)
  Willi. 16
Sessions, Alexandr. 30
Sever, Joshua 36
  Robert 15
Severanc, Ephraim 37
Sexton, Giles 10
  Gyles 11
Seyle, Franc. 17
Shaflin, Michaell 19
Shaller, Michaell 38
Shaperd, John 35
Shapleigh, Niccolas 23
Sharman, John 15
Sharpe, Rich. 29
  Samll. 10, 11
Shattuck, William 37
Shaw, Jno., jun. 32
Shawe, Abraham 15
  Joseph 16, 40
  Roger 16
Shead, Daniel, juni. 37
Shearman, Jno. 26
Shefeild, Edmo. 20
Sheilden, Thomas 39
Shelden, Isack, junr. 39
  Jno. 33
  Tho. 32
Sheopard, Edwa. 20
Shepard, Solomon 37
Shephard, John 20
  Tho. 31
Shepheard, John 22
  Samll. 14
  Tho. 14
Sheprd., Jer. 32
Sheratt, Hugh 13
Sherman, Abiah 35
  Edmond 14
  Phillip 12
  Samu. 18
Shoare, Sampson 28
Shore, Sampson 19
Short, Hen. 30
Shorte, Henry 13
Shortridg, Rich. 28
Shrimpton, Samuel 28
Shrires, Jerre. 22
Sibley, John 13
  William 36
Sibly, Sam. 36
Sike, Vickry 31
Sill, John 16
Silvester, Rich. 10
  Richard 12
Simonds, Benj. 37
Singletery, Richrd. 16
Skelton, Samll. 10, 11
Skerry, Francis 15
  Henry 15
Skiner, Thomas 38
Skinner, Tho. 22, 24

Thomas, jun. 35
Skot, John 17
Smaley, Francis 24
Smally, James 35
Smead, Wm. 31
Smeadley, Jno. 30
Smeedly, Baptize 20
  John 20
Smist, Tho., jun. 25
Smith, Abr. 27
  Abraham 27
  Asahail 35
  Chileab 28
  Frances 40
  Hemry 37
  Hugh 19
  James 23, 27, 32
  Jno. 24
  Jno., jun. 31
  John 21, 23, 27
  John John 38
  John Philip 38
  Jonathan 37
  Joseph 38
  Mathewe 20
  Mighil 21
  Nath. 26
  Nathan 32
  Nathani. 40
  Peletiah 31
  Richard 37
  Sam. 26, 30
  Saml. Chiliab 38
  Saml. Philip 38
  Samuel 39
  Samuell 40
  Tho. 29
  Willi. 20
  Wm. 28, 33, 35
Smyth, Beniamin 18
  Christo. 20
  Franc. 17
  Frauncs 11
  Henry 10, 11
  John 12
  Laurence 20
  Samll. 13
  Tho. 12
  Willm 14
Smythe, Francis 15
  Henry 16, 18
  John 14 (2), 15, 17
  Thomas 15
Snow, Jno. 29
Snowe, Thoma. 19
Somersbey, Antho. 19
  Henry 19
Somersby, Abiel 26
Southcoate, ---, Capt. 10
  Rich. 10
  Thomas 10
Souther, Joseph 33
  Nath. 22
Southick, Laurence 17
Southwell, William 39
Sparhauke, Nathani. 17
Sparhawk, Nathaniell 37
Sparhawke, Samuell 37
Spaulden, Edward 35
  John 35
Spencer, Gerret 15
  John 13
  Micha. 15
  Tho. 22, 32
  Thomas 12
  Willm 11
Spere, Geo. 20
Spinny, Tho. 22

Spoffard, Sam. 33
Spolden, Edward 18
Spooer, John 16
Spooner, Thom. 15
Sprage, Jno. 22
  Ralfe 10 (2)
  Rich. 11
Sprague, John, jun. 35
  Jonathan 35
  Phinehas 38
  Phinias 35
  Samuell, jun. 35
  Samuell, Left. 35
Sprauge, Jno. 24
Spring, Hen. 24
  Henary, junr. 37
Spurr, Robrt. 25
  Robt. 27
Spurrell, Christopher 23
Squire, John 34, 37
  Joseph 38
  Phillip 38
  Tho. 12
Stacy, Symon 26
  Wm. 31
Stacye, Hugh 19
Stamford, Tho. 24
Standige, James 17
Standley, Samuel, Corpr.
  36
Stanley, Christo. 18
  Tho. 13
  Tymothy 13
Staple, Abra. 29
  John 21
Starlinge, Wm. 32
Starns, John 37
Stebben, John 21
Stebbing, Joseph 32
Stebbins, Benjamin 39
  Benony 33
  Edm. 12
  Edward 39
  Samuel 39
  Thomas 39
Steedman, Robrt. 16
Steele, George 12
  John 12
Steephens, Jno. 26
Steevens, Henry 22
  Joseph 29
  Tho. 25
  Thomas 39
Stephenson, Andr. 20
Sterne, Isaacke 11
Sternes, Charles 21
  Isak 25
  Nathani. 22
Stevens, Jno. 25
  John 18, 19
  John, L. 37
  Willi. 17, 19
  William 35
Stickland, John 10
Sticknee, Tho. 34
Stickney, Sam. 33
  Willi. 18
Stidman, John 18
Stiels, John 39
Stileman, Elias 11, 19
Stilson, Willm 12
Stimson, John 20
  Jonathan 37
Stirt, Edward 23
Stoakes, Henry 29
Stocker, Ebenezer 40
Stockin, George 13
Stodard, Antho. 18

Stoddar, Sam. 30
Stoddard, Samson 38
  Simeon 38
  Solomon 28
Stoder, John 19
Stone, Dan. 20
  David 21
  Ebenezer 36
  Gregory 14
  Jno. 25
  Nath. 26
  Sam. 24, 32
  Samll. 12
  Symon 14, 22, 24
Story, Wm., jun. 27
Stoughton, Israell 12
  Tho. 11
  Thomas 10
Stover, Jno. 29
  Silvester 23
Stow, Nathanell 35
Stowe, John 13
  Sam. 20
  Tho. 22, 24
Stower, Nich 11
  Richard 22
Stowers, John 14
  Straite, Thomas 35
Strange, George 13
Stratten, Jno. 24
  Sam. 22, 24
  Samuell 35
Streete, Ste. 20
Strickland, ---, Srieant.
  10
Strong, Ebener. 33
  Jedediah 39
Stronge, John 15
Stubbs, Josua 21
Stuksley, Tho. 32
Sumer, George 24
  Incre. 31
  Wm. 30
Sumers, Henry 37
Sumner, Roger 24
  Samuel 37
  Willi. 15
Sutton, Lambrt. 20
Swaine, Jerimiah 40
Swan, Henry 17
  Jno. 26
  Richd. 33
  Richrd. 17
Swayne, Jno. 25
  Richrd. 16
  Willm 14
Sweete, John 19
Swetman, Thomas 16
Swetnam, Tho. 39
Swett, John 19
Swift, Obadiah 28
Swifte, Tho. 13
Swinaton, Job, Sergt. 36
Swinnerton, Job 17
Switzer, Sethe 16
Syckes, Richrd. 17
Sykes, Increas 33
Symes, Jno. 24
Symonds, Caleb 37
  John 15
  Marke 16
  Samu. 15
  Samuel 38
  Samuell 36
  Wm. 27
Symons, Henry 20
  Herlakenden 25
  Jno. 22

58

Syms, Sachariah 13
Syverens, John 15

--- T ---

Tabor, Phillip 12
Talcott, John 11
Talmage, Thomas 12
Talmidge, Willm 12
Tapley, Clement 17
Tappin, Abraham 16
  Rich. 12
Tarbell, John 36
Tarne, Miles 20
Tatman, John 15
Tayer, Thom. 21
Tayler, Abraham 36
  Edwa. 21
  Philip 19
  Richrd. 19
Taylor, Edw. 31 (2)
  George 16, 24
  Henry 25
  John 22, 33
  Richrd. 19
  Sebred 30
Taylour, Gregory 12
  John 10, 11
Tedd, Josua 16
Tell, William 35
Tempel, Abraham 35
  Isaac 35
  Recherd 35
Temple, Jno. 27
  Ric. 28
Terre, Stephen 11
Terree, Stephen 10
Thacher, Thom. 21
Thackster, Thom. 19
Thatcher, Peter 30
  Samu. 19
  Samuell 37
Thaxter, Sam. 31
Thayer, Nathanll. 38
Thing, Jno. 31
  Jnothan. 23
Thirston, Benj. 25
  Dani. 31
  Jno. 24
Thomas, Evan 18
  Hugh 22
  Joseph 39
  Rise 22
Thompson, James 29
  Jno. 22, 24, 28
  Wm. 24
Thorndick, Paul 31
Thorne, Willi. 16
Thorneton, Thomas 13
Thornton, Timo. 27
Thorp, Jams 35
Thorpe, Henry 21
Throckmrton., George 10
Throdingham, Will. 10
Thrumball, John 18
Thurlo, Franc. 27
Thurston, John 20
Thwing, Benja. 31
  Edw. 30
Thwinge, Benia. 20
Tiff, Willi. 18
Tiler, Mosis 39
Tileston, Timo. 25
Tilton, Abraham 32
Tinge, Edwrd. 18
Tinker, Jno. 23

Titcombe, Willi. 19
Toleman, Jno. 31
  Tho. 31
  Thom. 17
Toll, John 20
Tomkins, John, junr. 19
  John, senr. 19
  Ralph 15
Tomlyns, Edw. 11
  Tymothy 11
Tompson, Henry 27
  James 12
  John 13
  Symon 18
  Willi. 18
Tomson, Symon 21
Topliffe, Samuel 28
Topp, Mary 23
Toppan, Jacob 30
  John 25
Toppn, Bartho. 27
Torrey, Josiah 33
  Micajah 28
  Sam. 26
  Wm. 28
Torry, Willi. 19
Tory, Philip 20
Toule, Roger 20
Tounr., Jacob 34
Tower, John 16
Town, Peter 37
Towne, Willi. 15
Townes, Joseph, senr. 36
Townesend, Thomas 16
Townsend, Andrew 40
  James 27
  Jno. 31
  Pen 29
  Samll. 38
  Samll., jun. 38
  Samuel 33
  Tho. 33
  Will. 14
Toy, Wm. 24
Traske, Will. 10
Travis, Daniel 28
Treadway, Josiah 36
Tredwell, Nath. 32 (2)
  Tho. 32 (2)
  Thomas 16
Trescot, Willi. 20
Tresler, Thom. 19
Trick, Eljas 29
Triscot, Jno. 33
Tristram, Ralfe 23
Trot, Thom. 20
Trott, Symon 23
  Thomas, junr. 37
Trout, Wm. 29
Trow, Hen. 30
Trowbridge, James 25
True, Joseph 37
Truesdale, Sam. 34
Trull, John, senr. 37
Trumbell, John 17
Trumble, Jno. 25
  Joseph 32
Trusedale, Rich. 13
Tucke, Robert 17
Tucker, Ephr. 31
  Jno. 28, 30 (2)
  Manasses 31
  Meros 37
Tuffes, Peter 31
Tuffs, Peter 25
Tuffts, Jonathan 35
  John 35
Tuisdale, Jno., junr. 23

Tuisdall, Jno., senr. 23
Tuksbery, Henry, senr. 39
Turbat, Peter 23
Turill, Daniel 26
Turner, Eph. 26
  Jeffry 20
  Jno. 26
  John 21
  Nath. 10, 11
  Robte 12
  Willi. 20
Turney, Benia. 18
Tuttle, Edward 38
  Elisha 38
  Henry 15
  Jno. 27
  John 16, 38
  Jonathan 38
  Richard 14
Twelves, Robt. 24
Twitchwell, Joseph 12
Tybbot, Walter 19
Tydd, John 20
Tyler, Hope 29
  Hopstill 39
  John 39
Tylestone, Thomas 15
Tylley, John 13
Tyng, Jonathan 31
Tynge, Willm 16
Tytus, Robrt. 17

--- U ---

Uffott, Thomas 11
Umphryes, James 20
Underwood, Tho. 25
  Thomas 15
  Wm. 22
Undrhill., Jo., Capt. 10
Undrwood., Joseph 21
  Martyn 13
Undurwoode, Joseph 37
Upam, Nathaniell 35
  Phinias 35
Upham, John 14
  Nath. 22
  Nathan. 24
  Phineas 34
Upher, Hezechi. 16
Upsall, Nich. 10, 11
Uptan, John, senr. 40
Usher, John 28
Ustice, Joseph 38

--- V ---

Valentine, John 30
Vales, James 28, 33
Vallack, Nico. 29
Vane, Henry, Esq. 14
Vauhan, Wm. 26
Venner, Thomas 15
Vereing, Phillip 14
Veren, Philip 18
Vermaes, Benia. 19
Viall, John 19
Vickery, Jnoth. 31
Vickrey, Iseck 32
Vincen, Willi. 20
Vining, Jno. 25
Vose, Robrt. 25
Vyol, Jno. 33

60

Whitton, James 24
Widger, James 29
Wieth, John 37
  William 37
Wiggin, Thomas 26
Wight, Danll. 35
  Eph. 28
  Henry 21
  Jno. 22, 24
  Joseph 31
  Sam. 28
Wiglesworth, ---, Mr. 31
Wignall, Alex. 10, 11
Wilboare, Samll. 12
Wilcocks, Willi. 14
Wilcockson, Willi. 14
Wildar, Thom. 18
Wilder, Edwa. 20
WildGoose, Jno. 29
Wilely, Timothy 40
Wilkins, Benja. 36
  Bray 12
  Henry 36
  John 28
  Richard 38
  Tho., senr. 36
Willard, Sam. 27
  Symon 31
Willes, Michaell 16
Williams, George 12
  Hugh 19
  Natha. 18
  Rob. 20
  Robrt. 15
  Samuell 22
Willington, Benjamin 36
  Palsgrave 37
  Rodger 37
Willis, Edw. 28
  Edward 28, 33
  George 16
  Laurenc. 26
  Nicho. 32
Willjams, Abr. 25
  Isack 34
  Natha. 30
  Niccolas 22
  Thomas 23
Willms, Roger 10, 11
  Tho. 11
  Thomas 10
Willoues, Steven 25
Willoughby, Franc. 17
Wills, Thom. 16
Willson, ---, Left. 35
  Nathaniell, senr. 36
Willust, Jo. 11
  Nicholas 13
Wilson, Gowen 22
  Henry 18
  Jacob 18
  John 10, 11, 21
  John, senr. 37
  Joseph 15, 34
  Sam. 34
  Theophi. 16
  Thomas 12
  Will. 14

Wilton, David 12
Wincall, Robte 13
Winchester, Alexandr. 14
  John 15
Wincoll, Jno. 22
  John 21
Windsor, Joshua 30
Wines, Faintnot 20
Wing, Joseph 31
Wingat, Jno. 28
Winge, Jos. 31
Winn, Edwa. 20
Winship, Ephraim 31
  Ephrajm 32
Winshipp, Edw. 13
Winslad, Jacob 35
Winsley, Samu. 16
Winslow, Jno. 27
Winthrop, ---, Major
  Genl. 38
  Adam 33
  Deane 25
  John, junr. 11
  Wait, Maj. General 34
Winthrope, Adam 18
  John, jun. 14
  John, sen. 14
  Steven 14
Wise, Nicho. 20
Wisewall, Ichabod 29
  John 16
  Tho. 22
Wiswall, Ebenezr. 30, 31
  John 38
  Noah 34
Witchfield, John 12
Withe, Nicks. 35
Withengton, Henry 30
Witheredge, Edwa. 20
Witherell, John 19
Withers, Tho. 22
Withington, Ebenezer 37
  Phillep 37
  Richrd. 17
Withman, John 19
Witt, Walltar 39
Wjer, Peter 23
Wms, Ebenezr. 33
Wms., Robt. 27
Wody, Richrd. 19
Wood, Abraham 36
  Daniel 39
  Daniell 36
  Ellis 28
  John 17, 35
  Josiah 37
  Michaell 17
Woodberry, Willi. 18
Woodbery, Hump. 31
  Isa. 31
  Jno. 27
  Nicho. 28
Woodbury, John 10, 11
  Peter 26
  Tho. 33
Wooddey, Hen. 24
Wooddy, Richrd. 20

Woode, Edward 17
  John 20
  Nicho. 18
Woodford, Thomas 13
Woodman, Archelaus 15
  Edward 14
  Jno. 26
  Jonathan 39
Woodmansey, John 28
Woods, James 38
  John, Ens. 40
  Willm 11
  Wm. 36
Woodward, Amos 30
  Geo. 21
  Jno. 31
  John 36, 40
  Nathani. 15
  Peter 19
  Ralph 15
  Richard 14
Woodworth, Henry 20
Woolcott, Henry 10
Woolfe, Peter 12
Woolridge, John 10, 12
Woolson, Thomas 36
Worcester, Samuel 27
  Willi. 17
Worde, Thom. 19
Wormestall, Arthur 23
Worth, John 39
Wray, Danll. 12
Wriford, John 29
Wright, Abel, senr. 39
  Ebenezer 39
  Henry 13
  Jno. 25
  John 20, 37
  Joseph 29, 39
  Judah 30
  Rich. 12
  Sam. 33
  Samu. 21
  Samuel 39
Wthrington, Jno. 28
Wulcott, Henry 12
  John 13
Wyat, Edwa. 20
Wyman, Jacob 37
  Jonathan 37
  Seth 37
  Will. 37
Wynes, Barnaby 13

--- Y ---

Young, Rowland 23
Younglove, Jno. 30
  Sam. 27

--- Z ---

Zullesh, David 19

www.ingramcontent.com/pod-product-compliance
Lightning Source LLC
Chambersburg PA
CBHW060615290326
41930CB00051B/2642